Edward Wright

graphic work & painting

D1477455

Preface *Joanna Drew*

In 1960 Edward Wright wrote that 'the heart of 20th century myth is the knowledge that each science, each activity is a part of all others . . .'. After an architectural training Wright has been a painter, typographer, graphic designer and above all an explorer of language. He was once described as the only artist in England who has used communications as his theme and at the centre of his work has been a continuing speculation about the meeting point between the visual sign and the meaning it carries.

In the early 1950s Wright taught experimental typography at the Central School and went on to teach at the Royal College of Art and finally to become head of graphics at Chelsea. The unique nature of his example is recorded in this catalogue by the designers Trilokesh Mukherjee, Theo Crosby and Ken Garland, all of whom benefited from his guidance. We have also taken the opportunity of gathering together several pieces of writing by Edward Wright published in various journals over the years.

We are extremely grateful to Edward Wright for the time and patience he has devoted to this exhibition and to the design of its catalogue and publicity material. We have been helped throughout by the advice of Trilokesh Mukherjee who proposed the project to us. Our warm thanks are due to him, the other authors, lenders of works and everyone who has helped us in the research and preparation of the exhibition.

Acknowledgements *EW/MH*

Many people have contributed in various ways to the making of this exhibition. The scholar and bibliophile Antonio Carrizo, Maria Abdelnour, Trilokesh Mukherjee, Jorge Perez-Román and John Pym all helped in finding material for the *codex atorrantis*; Mark Lumley helped in its completion and David Yandell devised its display. Molly Izzard provided guidance on the 'Learning' section of the autobiographical 'The Elm Tree'. Pavel Büchler and Michael Coles advised on the design and typography of the catalogue. Others including several of those listed as lenders at the back of this catalogue have given advice and information. We should like to thank them all.

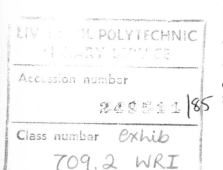

The example of Edward Wright   *Trilokesh Mukherjee*

Edward Wright *is* my teacher, and he will always
remain my teacher. This is not because we have both
grown since we first met and therefore logically I can't
catch him up, which is true. Neither is it because I have
an orientalist attitude of reverence to my teacher (a
person to whom debts cannot be repaid) and I owe to
him my understanding of life and my present livelihood,
which is also true. But it is because of the discoveries I
have made about Edward through my experiences of
him and other teachers, designers and human beings.
The discoveries which made me realise that he is quite
different. It is difficult to define the difference, but I
know that I will always have a lot to learn from him.
Life is so gloriously unpredictable. In 1963 I made a
difficult choice of not going on to study sculpture
(which first attracted me to Chelsea School of Art)
under Fullard and Frink, and deciding to study
graphic design under Edward Wright who until then
was just a vague name to me. I well remember our
meeting. After going through a test for life-drawing,
two tests for the History of Art (three hour written, and
an hour of slide-test) and a day-long test for graphic
design, I was called for the interview. I was no longer
apprehensive but did not at all expect to meet a pair of
sharp though inquisitive and yet gentle eyes which
betrayed that they saw more than what was on the
surface. He explained the new course structure and, as
he was explaining to me what graphic design is, the
penny suddenly dropped. So it was to do with the visual
world of meanings and it was to do with an
understanding of a discipline with rules, history and
humanity. Of course at the beginning his teaching
method did not strike us as different. Ignorant as we
were, we thought that was how design was taught
everywhere. I had no idea about the subject and
naturally I had no idea about how it was taught. It was
only when my friends on other courses in other colleges
started questioning why I bought such obscure books as
Piaget's *The Language and Thought of the Child* and *The
Child's Conception of Numbers*, Ozenfant's *Foundations
of Modern Art*, Le Corbusier's *Le Modulor*, or
Eisenstein's *The Film Sense* that I realised that we were
being exposed to a slightly different world of
experience.

When I look back on those early days of Chelsea's

photograph by Tim Highmoor

Paolozzi in Chelsea 1965
photograph by Lynn Fishman

Graphic Design Department it amazes me how we loved the life there. We had no cameras (we all bought our own), we had no printing press (we all bought Adanas), we had no giant projector (we used squared-up proportion for enlargement). We lived an extraordinary life. We hardly ever missed a day. We lived, experienced, went swimming together (after discovering that the super-bureaucratic Edward's companion portable typewriter was only a case containing his swimming trunks), photographed Paolozzi in his studio or Colin St John Wilson's house at Cambridge, visited the hand-made paper firm at Barcham Green, Kent, or walked up the narrow steps to Lawrence's of Bleeding Heart Yard to discover Japanese handmade paper and cherry wood blocks for engraving. We hung 20' long concrete poems at the Brighton Poetry Festival, or made masks and photographed each other in Epping Forest. Nothing was taboo. We went to hear Anthony Froshaug talking about typography and Ulm, Godo Iommi came to read Spanish poems and play tapes of a metal-cast poem being read as it was nailed on a rock by the sea at Horcón in Chile as the waves splashed. We went on bitter-cold days to draw in Brixton and discovered hot Jamaican meat pie at Joe's shop.

Once I went through one of those crises of youth and did not feel like working at all. I still went to the college every day, that was my only anchor. My fellow students left me alone. My teachers and Edward left me alone. After about three weeks, one lunchtime when I was sitting alone in the classroom looking vacantly at the fire-brigade practising, I felt a hand on my shoulder. 'I am rather hungry and feeling a bit lonely as well. I wonder whether you would like to join me for lunch.' I looked up and hesitated. He smiled, took away all my defence and said 'you will do me a favour old chap'. We had a Chinese meal at the *Rice Bowl* (he always had prawn curry and rice) and then walked along the river before Edward lit his cigarette and said 'Do you think it matters whether they paint or don't paint the Chelsea Bridge?' We discussed and argued. Halfway through this discussion he smiled and said that I was not contributing much to the class, and he and the other students missed it. This normalised me.

Godo Iommi reading a poem 4 miles off the coast of Chile, at Horcón

Later, after leaving Chelsea, I spent some time trying to

find out about how to teach graphic design. I went round to various schools of design in England and abroad. I met various design teachers either asking them how they teach or sitting in their classes to understand how they teach. The experience was slightly superficial because the time spent was not enough. But it was sufficient to make me realise the qualities of Edward's teaching. I now consider him as one of the great design teachers. Not everybody will agree with me but it does not really matter. My other heroes in this field are Hoffman, Gurtler, Glaser, Albers, Kapitski, Krampen, Hollenstein and Mandel. Of these I have met some. Others are known to me either through their students or through their writing. What these people have in common is a vision which they were able to share joyfully with their followers. They have the ability to instil in their students' minds the idea of what E. M. Forster so simply calls 'only connect'. We have eyes to see. The world is full of visual signs and images. Some exist naturally. Some are made by us. Through pre-conditioning we discover the meanings of these signs. Edward was forever telling us about the Incas, and the Mayas about the Indians of South America, their marks, their traditions. Sometimes as creative persons we impose meanings on marks we make. Through marks made on rocks, sands, papers, CRT screens, WC walls, or on printed books we are trying to say something. We use language. We communicate. Edward was interested in semantics, anthropology, psychology, painting, sculpture, architecture, music, film, photography, history . . . it was quite incredible. I sometimes went to his house (the added attraction was always Kitty's cooking) and found him busy with the problems of lighting on a plaster-cast he had just done. Sometimes he would spend hours trying to translate van Ostaijen's writing. All the time filling his notebooks with notes, sketches, ideas. Sometimes over the weeks I have seen an idea grow. While working Edward became tense, rather silent, eyebrows often meeting, not smiling, drinking a lot of coffee and smoking cigarettes, and then finally the ever generous, smiling Edward would hold a print of a woodcut already signed, ready for me to take back. You never knew what you would come away with from his house. Sometimes it was a director's chair, sometimes a marble slab, sometimes it was Canetti's *Crowds and Power* or Levi-Strauss's

ama
eme
amie
noe
nunu
uyu
aya
yva
vere
ire
ora
huir
urde
yuyo
arde
yeta
ira
ola
ojo
uva
yace
hace
echa
hilo
jira
oca
surte
yerba
ala
verde
flecha
tire
roe
tueca
sayo
caza
zaga
ese
cilla
mozo
mueve
yugo

Vowel poem by Edward
Wright, Chelsea School of Art
c 1968

Structural Anthropology. In those days I had no idea who
Canetti or Levi-Strauss was. Also Picasso. Edward saw
something in Picasso that we did not see. I suppose it
was Picasso's ability to break the so-called rules and still
give a perfectly acceptable and exciting account of
himself. And, of course, Picasso was Catalan, spoke
against Franco. It is really the vision Edward had of the
world, a somewhat conscientious and moral vision, full
of excitement, full of discoveries, and, above
everything, it was his ability to see and indeed show us
the extraordinariness of a trivial object. He would stick
an orange wrapper or an olive-oil can up on the wall
and talk with excitement of the colour, typography,
spacing, but above all the image. The iconography
interested him deeply.

Later I had the opportunity to assist him in a few design
projects. Whether it was lettering for buildings (Hinsley
House, New Scotland Yard), typography for a leaflet, or
a poster he always managed to evoke in the job and in
me a strange combination of precision and romanticism
all at the same time. After spending hours drawing a
letter-form, I would then spend hours making and
polishing balsa wood models for bronze-casting. His
method of simplifying a problem so that we can see the
skeleton before starting to work was a lesson for me.

I remember reading a passage by Camus, 'Do not walk
in front of me, I may not follow. Do not walk behind
me, I may not lead. Just walk beside me and be my
friend.' As I started teaching myself Camus's words
became an important guide to me. I realised that for a
good teacher the challenge is how to make sure that the
student discovers for himself or herself and learns to
become an independent thinker and an independent
interpreter of events, objects or mark. All the time
making sure we never forget that we are primarily
human beings and that the human relationship, the
history, the culture, the person, are more important
than a profession. A teacher's job is not to create a
miniature version of a teacher but to open windows and
doors of minds, and let light and fresh air come in. And
in the joy of discovering that novelty the student
realises that he or she really knew it all along. To train a
person for a job is not an easy task. To educate is a
more demanding task. To inform and increase one's

knowledge of facts is, I believe, a relatively easy task. To make someone think independently and to make someone wiser is an achievement of a good teacher. I think Edward is, for me, one of those very rare educators.

Sadly 'Art' as a subject has been continually fragmented and compartmentalised. And it is an easy temptation to put Edward in the cubby hole of a graphic designer or typographer. I'm not a statistician. I see him as an artist and a teacher. There have been moments when he was humble enough to tell me that I have taught him something. That also is indeed his own greatness to acknowledge even a minute experience. But to me it always is a humbling experience. I never understood how one can use a past tense about a teacher. I certainly never have felt that he *was* my teacher. He *is* my teacher and he always will be.

Trilokesh Mukherjee at Chelsea
summer 1977
photographs by Lesley Hamilton

Painting, graphic work and an absent book *Michael Harrison*

We are only here on earth to dream
to leave a few illuminated manuscripts
                          like dreams.
The pottery of the Toltecs lies beneath the ground
scattered like the petals of flowers.

We have painted the heart of heaven upon deerskin
but will those who come after comprehend the Codex?

Ernesto Cardenal[1]

Jorge G. Marcos with a
burial pot, uncovered in
the Valley of Chanduy,
coast of Ecuador,
summer 1970

1. *Quetzal feathers dry – in time*
from *Cantares Mexicanos I*,
translated from the Spanish
by Roger Pring-Mill, Search
Press, London.

2. Wright describes this work as
that of a *bricoleur* or 'odd job
man'. In post war years
'one learnt to "cannibalise"
things and turn them into
what one needed, as for
example, the mouldings and
glass from bombed-out
houses which became
framing materials for an
exhibition of drawings at the
Mayor Gallery.'

In 1970 Edward Wright made a journey to Peru, Chile
and Ecuador, returning after thirty years to the
countries of his late parents. From that visit he brought
back a few photographs, taken with a borrowed camera,
of an archaeological dig.

These photographs were among the first things which
Edward Wright showed me. Before meeting him I had
seen a collage, a woodcut and some of his graphic
design work. Paintings were scattered and much had
been lost or destroyed, but I then set out to visit people
who owned pictures, all of whom had memories of
Edward Wright at various stages of his career.
Gradually, as an archaeologist might, I began to put
together fragments which were puzzling in isolation.

The most solid evidence was to be found in the
notebooks which Edward Wright has kept since 1953:
hand-made books of vegetable parchment (though the
first is of newsprint), 10 × 6 × an inch thick, each bound
in hessian with Japanese end-papers. The first
contains two self-portraits: one a doubting, worried
mirror-image; the other not a face, but an arm in the
act of drawing itself – a self-portrait of someone
conscious of his activity as a maker.

Wright, at this time, was a painter, but also, with post-
war scarcities, a designer and a maker.[2] His first
exhibition at the Mayor Gallery had been of ink and
gouache drawings of useful objects and, at a time when
contemporaries were entering maquettes to the
competition for a *Monument to the Unknown Political
Prisoner*, Wright was making a sculpture of the
Metamorphosis of a Gas Ring. There was mischievous
irony in this but also a genuine interest in the things we
make and use as expressions or emblems of our
existence. In the early '50s Wright designed cane
mannequins for Simpsons of Piccadilly and that first
notebook includes diagrams for a lampstand and a type

9

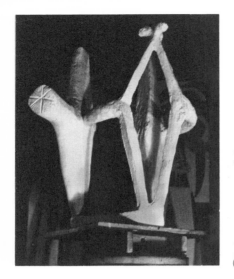

Gas ring reed pen drawing 1948

Metamorphosis of a Gas Ring plaster 1949 (destroyed)

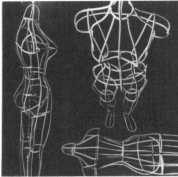

Three cane mannequins

bench. It was force of economics that made Wright seek work in an advertising agency while he saw himself primarily as a painter, but there was also a conviction that these activities, and their products, were not separate. 'Domestic appliances, advertisements, and people's everyday gestures need not be placed in a caste system below that which includes sculptures, easel pictures and mime. We can't withhold feelings for special occasions and at the same time keep them alive.'[3]

What also can clearly not be separated from the rest is Edward Wright's work as a teacher — not of painting but, significantly, of graphic communication. The first notebook has pages outlining exercises in typographical experiment which he developed in the evening classes at the Central School and other teaching projects crop up subsequently. But often, even when not concerned with teaching, the notes are those of an auto-didact, urging and admonishing, setting down an idea in slogan form to test its validity, going back to correct a previous thought — each note given its date.

The first image of the first notebook is a diagram showing where each letter sound is produced in the mouth. A print which Wright made many years later announced 'the gesture goes before the word', and here he is found exploring the physiological gestures which produce the sounds which in turn make up the spoken word. Wright is again interested in the apparatus. There follows a series of *'teste typografice'*, culminating in the painting *at A* which originally had letters floating inside and outside the head, a metaphor for the head which hears and thinks and speaks.

Page from a notebook — typographic heads

3. 'The Painter', *The Arts, Artists and Thinkers*, Longmans, Green and Co. 1958.

Compositional drawing

Page from a notebook 7.8.57

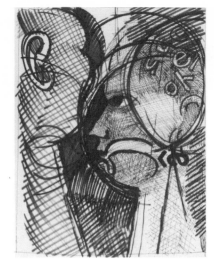

Page from a notebook –
Which is the sign?

Throughout the first and second notebooks drawings take up the theme of conversation and the means of communication. There are compositional drawings for paintings which were to include telephones and musical instruments, but there is also a page on which Edward Wright notes something written by Braque about the development of Cubism:

'There was no question of starting from an object: we went towards it. And what concerned us was the path one had to follow in order to be able to go towards objects! . . . I was unable to introduce objects until I had created space.'

This note seems to coincide with an increasing feeling on Edward Wright's part that if he is to make images about the elusive and immaterial nature of human communication he must discard illustration of its hardware in favour of more graphic means. Some drawings of the *at A* kind had brought together two heads enclosed in keyhole-like shapes and there followed a series of paintings of crowds made up of stencilled keyhole heads. In some of these, entitled *Spectators,* a pair of cardboard 3-D glasses (the kind given out at cinemas at that time) has been used repeatedly as a stencil. These are crowds of watchers, present at the event of our looking at them, uniform and anonymous. The series was in part prompted by a painting Wright had made having looked at pebbles on the beach at Aldeburgh and the pun of that would not have escaped him. The individual dissolves into the crowd and in a notebook drawing the outlines of overlapping discs form hieroglyphs and the question is jotted down – 'Which is the sign?'[4]

4. 'I also had a good look at Capogrossi about this time as he invented a sign or emblem of sorts something like a hand or fork with which he did all manner of things in painting, eventually forming a kind of pictorial surface.' From a letter.

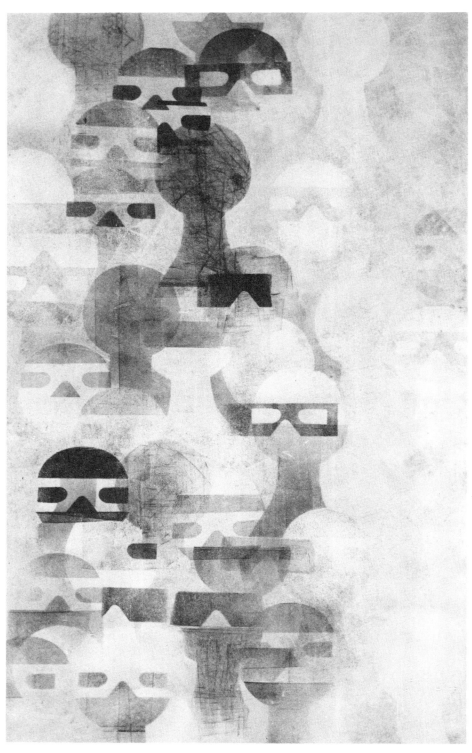

Spectators: Crowd 1957

Page from a notebook

Typographic experiment by
Germano Facetti at the
Central School 1952

Page from a notebook –
portrait sketch of Professor
Richard Guyatt, RCA

Blockprinted (wood letter)
pennant for *Groucho*, the motor
scooter of Cécile Villatte

As someone concerned with the means of
communication Wright has been fascinated to the point
of obsession with the meaning which marks can offer,
whether by intention or incidentally. A portrait sketch
of Richard Guyatt is as much an orchestration of
gestures (or signs) as the autographs of a group of
Kabuki actors which Wright collected in the back of the
first notebook. In his article 'Writing and the
Environment' he traced the evolution of writing from
pictograms to the development of alphabets, not just in
terms of their graphic qualities but also considering
their capacity for communication. 'Marks that were
made on a surface', he observed, 'were originally
ritualistic rather than descriptive'. This had been his
own experience as well in the bureaucratic procedures
of his father's office which had all the mystique of
incomprehensible meaning and importance.

At the Central School he encouraged students to use
letters freed for a while from their function as mere
components of words, each with their particular
meaning, but instead as 'elements of structure and
movement (later on of sound and image)'. He was
giving both the letters and his students the space to play
and breathe and explore their scope within the
discipline of a given process.

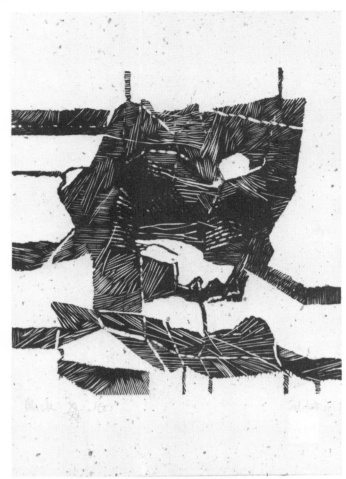

Mask woodcut 1963

Kuriquinga woodcut 1963

In his own work Edward Wright has valued the creative
element of play and the rules and rituals which a
process brings to the game. The technique of woodcut
printing reverses the norm of the gesture making the
mark: the black print records what is left after the
'drawing' has been cut. Which then is the mark? The
black or the white? In another sequence of prints an ink
roller is used to produce a frottage of paper clips and
other oddments: then that image is reversed
photographically. Being taught the technique of sugar
aquatint printing by Julian Trevelyan produced the
print *Touch*, in which an outlined hand reaches out
towards the raised braille letters T-O-U-C-H floating in
the dark labyrinth of a vast fingerprint.

Touch sugar aquatint 1958

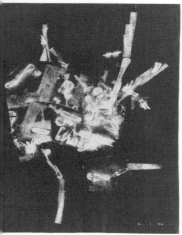

Photogram from ink
frottage 1956

Formalities collage 1957

Travelling collage 1959

Dialogue polyester resin
polychrome relief 1957

In his notebooks Edward Wright is constantly rewriting
the rules to fit closer to his purpose. Collage allows
fragments of things (not thrown away because they hold
some meaning) to jostle and interlock with each other,
to overlay, mask and obliterate. He was strongly
influenced by the collages of the Dadaists, but perhaps
more so by the clearly purposeful art of the Russian
Revolution. In April 1969 he wrote that the 'main
difference between collage I have made up to May of last
year (there has been a very long interval of years) and
anything I do now is to be found in a critical rejection
of exotic fragments. The pieces must say something in
themselves (however cryptic the sign) and contribute to
the main message (however cryptic and ambiguous that
may be).'

Life is a dream screenprint 1975

Poster for symposium on Latin
American culture 1974 –
Ariel Dorfman on 'Cultural
Repression in Chile'

Dreaming nevertheless
collage 1974

In some instances 'the main message' has been overt
political or social criticism. For if Edward Wright's
primary subject has been human communication, he
has a deeply held belief in our freedom to communicate
and a profound anxiety about its suppression and about
the power and abuse of modern communication
methods. In 'The Essential Book' he noted the French
author Charles Péguy comparing 'modern literacy to a
weary memory or a daily newspaper continuously
overprinted with pre-fabricated slogans'. Notebook

5. 'The Essential Book',
Icographic 5, 1973.

Agon screenprint 1975

Prisoners were held in the Chile Stadium in Santiago. The badge of the popular football team Colo Colo bears the head of the Araucanian hero Caupolican who resisted the Spanish invaders.

10 May 1933 Torchlight procession of students marches through Berlin to the University where an estimated 20,000 subversive books are burnt
Caption in AIZ: 'Thus spake Dr Goebbels: "Let us start new fires so that those who are blinded don't awaken"

451 screenprint

Page from a notebook 1953

drawings of 1953 have an ecclesiastical ape holding high a television aerial, cross-like, before a worshipping congregation, and, over the page, the Statue of Liberty brandishes an aerial instead of a torch, imprisoned by the winding flex. With the overthrow of Allende in Chile, however, humour gave way to outrage. A poster for a symposium on Latin American culture showed eyes, ears and mouth padlocked, the senses stopped, and in a screen-printed photo-collage the Statue of Liberty rears up again with the bitter words 'to live, to dream, to fabricate a phantom'.

'The atrocious, the absurd and bloodstained perversity of making a stadium into the antechamber of a slaughter house' provided Wright with an appalling ready-made juxtaposition for a second Chilean print. The third, *451*, links the burning of books which went on then with the book-burning of Nazi Germany and the destruction of the ancient Mexican codices by the invading Spaniards; each an attempt by an oppressive regime to erase history and memory.

The Cage oil painting 1949

at a oil painting 1955

de otras ciudades
Belén se encuentra en Barcelona
y un vago aparece como
duende ó sereno

of other cities
Bethlehem is found in Barcelona
and a tramp might be
a hobgoblin or a nightwatchman

codex atorrantinis

mi padre recordaba el casquillo
de un báculo golpeando la vereda
y confundiéndolo con la ronda
de un sereno le pidió la hora
al que se acercaba
el otro sin detenerse le contestó
viniendo de Nuestra Señora de
Belén en la Rambla
de los Estudios
" Cas cuatro me dieron
en Belén "

my father remembered the irony
of a stick striking the pavement
and taking it to be the nightwatch-
man's rounds he asked the approaching
man the time
the other without pausing
answered on his way from Our
Lady of Bethlehem in the Rambla
de los Estudios
' I heard four striking
at Bethlehem'

The idea for a new codex appears in the first notebook as part of the Central School teaching programme: like a Mexican codex in concertina form but 'applied to modern wrapping paper, one side only'. The notion lay dormant for many years but from 1972 its advances and vicissitudes are chronicled in the notebooks. Wright was working at that time on his article 'The Essential Book'. Péguy was the exemplary craftsman: for him 'a book meant a total commitment to social and spiritual truth. . . . A book meant writing, editing, printing, proof correcting, publishing and even opening a bookshop in the Rue de la Sorbonne' – the making and the message were inseparable.

The theme of the codex had been prompted by Wright's memory of his father recounting how one night in Barcelona he had heard 'the iron tip of a stick striking the pavement and, taking it to be the nightwatchman's rounds, he asked the approaching man the time. The other without pausing answered . . . I heard four striking in Bethlehem.'[6] The haunting image of Bethlehem in Barcelona stayed with him, with all its levels of memory, association, and inexplicable enigma. 'That man's memory will now have been obscured', he noted, 'four o'clock striking in a church named after

Screenprint 1976

6. Quoted from the screenprint *Codex atorrantinis* (above)

another city named after the mother of a family remembered a sacred birth a family without a house the birth in a stable.'

The codex was to be a 'narrative traced by wandering feet on any endless road', a book of the outcast. It's title *codex atorrantis* (originally misnamed *atorrantinis*) derived from the Buenos Aires underworld slang, *lunfardo*. *Atorrante*, the *lunfardo* word for a vagrant, had been coined from the name 'A. Torrent, the Anglo-Saxon drainage engineer who must be seen as part of this neo-colonialist process [and who] very fittingly produced quantities of pipes equally suitable for sewage and urban waste or as a refuge for the uprooted and exploited, or rather unexploitable being.'

In his article on Paul van Ostaijen, Edward Wright discussed the Belgian poet's use of Flemish rather than the literary French: 'language and theme are not to be separated because the substance with which his poems are made is speech'.[7] And similarly he found in Charles Péguy that the use of 'colloquial speech, the oral tradition, the idiom, from the printed page reached out to the heart'. *Lunfardo* was the natural language of the codex: a spoken language, born and changing of necessity, cryptic except to the outcast.

The codex was not, however, to have a single narrative. The concertina provided a sequence of pages but, when opened out, it allowed a synchronic reading. It was to be screen-printed with handwritten words but, soon after moving to Cambridge in 1977, Edward Wright bought a small proofing press and some type from printers who were changing to photo-setting and he switched to using letterpress. An idea of having woodcut illustrations was discarded. Themes and images which had been seminal would be dispensed with if too literal or bearing any trace of pathos. Footprints, 'the feet of the vagrant' and a favourite image since the 1950s, a still of Chaplin in *The Gold Rush*, the quotation from Brecht's *The Good Woman of Setzuan*, and even the starting point of '4 o'clock in Bethlehem' — one by one each was put aside.
In 1972 Wright had ruled: 'anything used must be documentary evidence and not fabricated artifice. The art lies in the sequence.' The presentation of words and

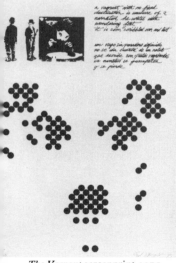

The Vagrant screenprint 1975

7. 'Paul van Ostaijen', *Typographica* 15, 1967.

Lettering on exhibition building International Union of Architects Congress,
South Bank, London 1961
Architect: Theo Crosby

Spectators: Wedding Guests oil
painting 1957

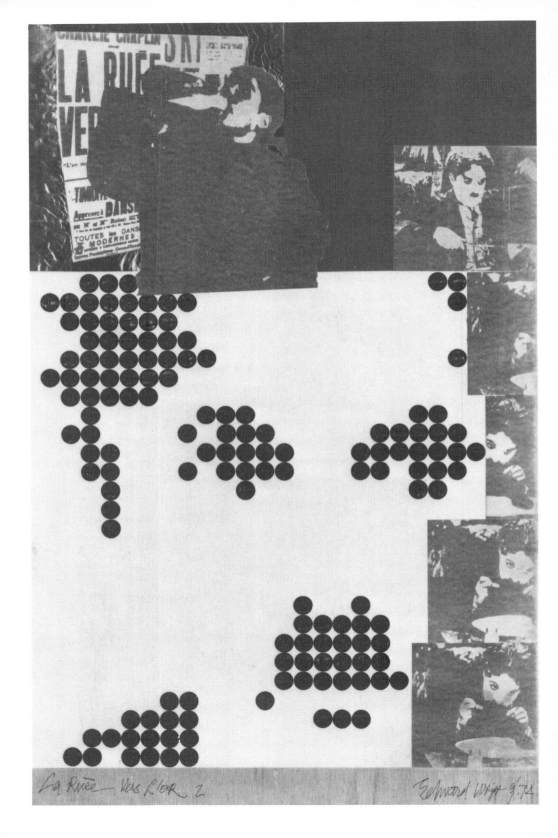

La Ruée Vers l'or 2   Edward Wright 9.74

La Ruée vers l'or 2 collage 1974
The image of Chaplin was
evolved as an exercise in
recognisability. For the
screenprint on page 21 Wright
opted for a diagonal grid.

images was to be utterly deadpan. Wright, like W. H. Auden, has always enjoyed lists of names and words, and in 1978 he opted for tabulated columns.[8] Listed alphabetically each word would be allowed to resonate in the company of others. Discovering that the Maori for 'book' is *puka puka* he decided to introduce other languages. In some instances the transformation of a word can be traced from language to language; in others a word can take on new meaning by association.

The codex moves dream-like from its glossaries (which were printed first) into images, each given a single word of *lunfardo*. The public aspirations and pretensions of a nation pictured in its postage stamps, themselves a kind of vernacular or common currency, are interspersed with an international anthology of the dispossessed. On the final spread the truant of Truffaut's *Les Quatre Cents Coups*, gulping the stolen milk (incidentally, against a poster for Chaplin's *The Gold Rush*), faces the floating travellers of the River Guayas, photographed by Edward Wright in 1938, who lived on the rafts of balsa logs which they brought down river to the timber yards of Guayaquil. 'Guayaquil', Wright has written, 'is a sacred and miraculous city. Indeed there are men who approach it from Daule walking upon the waters of the Guayas, is this not true? (They bring their houses with them.)'

This salvaged glimmer of autobiography is as poignant as the choice of language and the choice of theme. Coming from mixed Latin-American parentage, with a father in the consular service, and having spent crucially formative years in Ecuador and Chile, Wright is an exile wherever he is. His writing moves easily from English into Spanish but in one of the notebooks he remarks: 'I may understand and even speak foreign languages but I remain isolated.'

Printing was completed only in the spring of 1984 but several years ago Edward Wright had realized that the codex would be 'the absent book', that to fabricate this codex . . . requires that it should be in a certain sense the annotation, the commentary upon its real absent ghostly self . . . the codex is elsewhere . . . this is a commentary on it . . . the vagrant has moved off. . . .'

8. In one notebook Wright jots down 'Catrina's glossary', a list of his young grand-daughter's versions of various words. 'Chicken pox' becomes 'chicken socks', 'measles' becomes 'needles'.

Nonsense Conversation collage 1957

Pythagoras collage 1968

near Ickleton watercolour
studies 23.2.'81

With retirement Edward Wright and his wife Kitty
had moved to Cambridge to be nearer their
grandchildren. For the first time they owned a house
and a garden. The notebooks have continued and
watercolours map out this new territory and the water,
light and damp winds of the nearby Fens.

Wright had rediscovered watercolour in Chile in 1970.
He had been invited by the Catholic University of
Valparaiso but pre-election politics frustrated his
teaching programme, and so he bought watercolours
and paper and began to make pictures based upon
memories of the journey down the length of the Andes.
The paints travelled with him back up to Peru and
Ecuador and two watercolours, made after his return to
England, combine the image of a volcano-cum-pyramid
with a poem which speaks of 'the flux of rains of fire of
tears'. As 'the sky moving recognised its geometry
quartering the aprons of the pyramid', so could the
intangible and fugitive elements find their image in
watercolour. Wright recalled the insistence of Bert
Lupton, his teacher at Stonyhurst – 'Put it on and leave
it' – to allow chance and chemistry to combine with
gesture.

Cambridge garden
watercolour 21.5.'82

Watercolour II (Surface) 1963

Los Rios watercolour 1970

boi pustak biblos
kitab kniga kniha

livre liber
tokuhon
seisho

Codex atorrantis

The codex is printed by hand on brown ribbed kraft in black, in white and in other colours, on a proofing press. It is a single sheet of paper twenty feet long (6,10 m.); it is folded into a 10 × 10 inch format (255 × 255 mm.) of 24 pages. The edition is of 30 copies.

The *lunfardo* words which are listed with their various meanings, can be found in the following publications, which were given to me by Jorge Perez Román:

José Gobello & Luciano Payet: *Breve Diccionario Lunfardo*, 1959.
Carlos de la Púa: *La Crencha Engrasada.*
Alvaro Yunque: *La Poesia Dialectal Porteña*, 1961.
María Rosa Vaccaro: *Mataburro Lunfa*, 1976.

óc bók bouquin boekje

uch ksiazka pukapuka

ódigo codex

ode

Some of the images in the codex are taken from postage stamps (*parola* refers to the epic *Martin Fierro* by José Hernandez); others are taken from film stills in the National Film Archive: *atorro* (sleeping vagrants) is from Lionel Rogosin's documentary: *On the Bowery*, *ventana* is from Kurosawa's *Dodeska Den*, and *yirar* is from *les 400 coups* of Truffaut.

chamuyo (dossers sheltering in the portico of St. Paul's Covent Garden) is from a photograph taken by María Abdelnour. *pilcha* (a picture of Moondog) is from the sleeve of a record given to me by Don Hunstein. *yugo* is from a photograph, taken in 1938, of men rowing a balsa wood raft down the Guayas river to the port of Guayaquil.

EW

codex atorrantis

codex

codex atorrantis

---

boi pustak biblos
kitaƄ kniga kniha

bóc bók bouquin boekje
buch ksiazka pukapuka

livre liber
tokuhon
seisho

código codex
code

broli

chamuyo

águila	camambuses	otario	sombra
1 penniless 2 eagle	1 shoes 2 wild flowers	fool	1 jail 2 shade
alpiste	faso	percanta	tamango
1 alcohol 2 canary seed	cigarette	woman	shoe
atorrar	feite	pilcha	vento
sleep	scar	1 clothing 2 blanket	money
cachar	grela	queso	yirar
grab	woman	1 foot 2 sock 3 cheese	roam
cafúa	lunfardo	rúa	yugo
jail	1 argentine slang 2 thief	street	work

atorrante	atorro	bagayo	caminantes
croto		balurdo	
linyera		fangote	fanguses
poligriyo	apoliyo		tamangos
reo			tarros
vagrant	sleep	bundle	shoes

atorro

lastre

ventana

vento

pilcha

percanta

abanico
1 door 2 watchman 3 fan

broli
book ('libro')

chamuyo
conversation

chapar
take hold of

chirusa
girl

lampar
1 give 2 hand over 3 pay

lastre
food

lengue
handkerchief

leones
1 trousers 2 lions

linyera
1 bundle 2 immigrant 3 vagrant

mistongo
shabby

ñapar
1 grab 2 steal

paica
woman

ragú
hunger

sapo
1 padlock 2 toad

shuca
pocket

tarro
1 shoe 2 good luck 3 jar

tumba
1 boiled meat 2 prison food 3 tomb

ventana
1 eye 2 window

yeta
bad luck

lunfardo	spanish	french	italian	portuguese	english
buyón	sopa	bouillon	brodo	caldo	broth
canasta	prisión	prison	prigione	prisão	prison
chorro	ladrón	voleur	ladro	ladrão	thief
parola	palabra	parole	parola	palavra	word
ragú	hambre	faim	fame	fome	hunger
trabajo	robo	vol	furto	roubo	theft
yugo	trabajo	travail	lavoro	trabalho	work

parola

grela

yirar

yugo

Argot
Before the seventeenth century the word *argot* was
applied to the community of beggars who lived around
the Cours des Miracles in Paris. Later it came to mean
their slang, a secret code invented to protect the
community from intruders who might try to control
their activities. Such codes proliferate in synonyms.
Words overheard become obsolete when the meaning is
divulged, and new words must be found to replace
them. The technicalities of wrongdoing also promote a
terminology. A pickpocket can use a variety of names
for pockets in a garment to be frisked or raided. This is
what happens in the *lunfardo* slang of Buenos Aires.

Lunfardo
At the end of the last century in Buenos Aires, thieves
used to call themselves *lunfardos*. As with *argot*,
lunfardo or *lunfa* came to mean the secret code.
Synonyms proliferated and there are many words for a
single meaning. The depressed outer suburbs or *arrabal*
of Buenos Aires has its own slang and a literature, but
in the opinion of Borges it has a poor vocabulary and
lacks substance.[1] *Lunfardo* was gradually decanted into
arrabalero slang to enliven it. Many tango lyrics are
peppered with *lunfardismos*, as in the interpretations of
Carlos Gardel.[2] Most tangos have a theme of nostalgia,
but Gardel also recorded quite a few of what is known
as the *tango reo*,[3] with a *lunfardo* vocabulary.

Semantic development
The *lunfardo* vocabulary is formed by borrowing, by
inventing and by disguising words. What may be called
a semantic development corresponds to borrowing a
word from Spanish or another language and giving it a
new meaning. *Alpiste* in *lunfardo* means whisky or
alcohol; the same word in Spanish means canary seed;
the *lunfardo* word *alpiste* presumably means that it is a
stimulant for song. *Abanico* in *lunfardo* can mean door
or watchman according to context. In Spanish this word
means fan. The *lunfardo* word is a metaphor for the
implied opening and shutting. *Percanta* is one of a
variety of *lunfardo* words for woman; the meaning
comes from the Spanish *percala* (*percale*) which is a
close-textured linen dress fabric. *Ragú* in *lunfardo*
means hunger, which derives from the French *ragoût*,
meaning stew. *Tarro* in *lunfardo* can mean either boot

La Crencha Engrasada
by Carlos de la Púa

or good luck, according to context. The Spanish *tarro* means a cylindrical vase or jar. The *lunfardo* word pictures the boot as a container for a foot.

Phonetic development
Atorrante in *lunfardo* means a vagrant. The phonetic derivation comes from A. Torrent, the name of a nineteenth century sewage contractor who used to stack his concrete pipes on waste land near the port of Buenos Aires. Vagrants used the sewage pipes as sleeping quarters and became known as *A. Torrents* or *atorrantes*; by extension the word *atorro* came to mean sleep. Another *lunfardismo* is *croto*, which has the same meaning. Camilo Crotto (1864–1936) was a Governor of Buenos Aires who allowed unemployed day labourers to travel free on goods trains. *Dequera!* in *lunfardo* is a warning 'look out!' derived from the English 'take care'. There are phonetic derivations from *argot*, from Quichua and from Araucano. *Chucho* which means fear comes from the Quichua word for earthquake: *chhucchu*.

Anagrams
Disguised words in *lunfardo* are known as *vesre* (= revés = reverse). The first syllable is shifted to the end to camouflage the meaning. It is a similar device to Cockney rhyming slang or backslang.[4] The *lunfardo* word *broli* is the *vesre* of the Spanish *libro*, meaning book. Sometimes there are irregular syllabic reversals; a *lunfardo* word for trousers is *lompa*. The Spanish word *pantalón* = *talonpán* = *talonpa* = *lompa*. The *vesre* of *tango* is *gotán*.

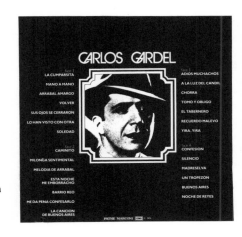

1. Jorge Luis Borges: *El idioma de los Argentinos* 1935.
2. Simon Collier: *The Tango made flesh: Carlos Gardel* (*History Today*) 1980.
3. *Yira Yira & Chorra*: Discepolo & Gardel. Odéon 1961. *Reo* means vagabond in this context.
4. Peter Mayer (in a letter) backslang: *ecilop* = police.

The Elm Tree   *Edward Wright*

Learning

'*Pedir peras al olmo*', my father used to say, which is 'to ask the elm tree for pears'. He meant that reliable results or 'pears' from somebody, or the 'elm tree' in question, would probably not be forthcoming. Sometimes I became the elm tree, but on one occasion I also acquired some early notions on the nature of printing. From 1922 to 1930 I was at boarding school, at Stonyhurst College, and sometimes during the school holidays I accompanied my father, Eduardo Wright Aguirre[1] to the Ecuadorian Consulate in Brunswick Street. Liverpool in those days was a very busy port with a large trade in imported and exported merchandise. This meant that when the Consulate was handling invoices, bills of lading and so forth, there was a variety of seals, rubber stamps and embossing dies being applied to the documents and I took a fancy to this type of graphic equipment. However, there was also a much more serious apparatus consisting of a book press and a leather and linen bound folio with numbered blank pages of tissue paper. It was used for the copying of letters written to the Ecuadorian equivalent of the Board of Trade or the Foreign Office. My father would have the letter typewritten, add his calligraphic signature and the appropriate consular seals, and then show me how it could be reproduced in the folio volume. A sheet of clean blotting paper was very slightly dampened and inserted into the folio with a waterproof card to isolate the page from its neighbours. The folio went into the press and the levers were turned, it was taken out and the letter was placed under the slightly humid page of tissue and it was returned to the press and again the levers were turned and when it was taken out of the book press, a perfectly legible facsimile of the letter left its impression on the numbered page. The day my father allowed me to use the book press, I overdid the dampening and the pressure and to his horror obtained a rather Chinese landscape – *décalcomanie* effect on the page and in addition, ruined the letter; I rather liked it, but had to admit that it would have to be done again. In addition the page of tissue became an embarrassment; if it were torn out, its absence would be noticed as it was numbered.

Years later I had to write a review for Herbert Spencer's *Typographica* 2 (New series, December 1960) on Richard

Fr. Richard Mangan S. J. and the class of Syntax I, Stonyhurst, summer 1929 (Wright is seated on the ground in front of Fr. Mangan)

1. Eduardo Wright Aguirre came from Guayaquil to Liverpool as Vice-Consul of Ecuador in 1902; he married Nellie Bunster Garrigó. My mother was the daughter of the Chilean Consul, Don Onofre Bunster. When I was six months of age, my father was appointed Consul of Ecuador in Barcelona. where we lived for four years. We returned to Liverpool in 1917, where my brother Thomas was born in 1920. In 1932 my father was appointed Chargé d'Affaires of the Ecuadorian Legation in London.

2. The documents in the box follow no particular order, although they usually have some bearing on the Large Glass, and faithfully reproduce the original paper upon which they were written or drawn (graph-printed school exercise book, buff drawing, grey blue letter, and yellowish tracing papers) with the original contours and irregularities. It appears that the material accumulated in a drawer over a period extending approximately from 1915 to 1923 and was then gathered up and copied exactly. So exactly that the box exerts a very coherent effect and can assimilate even the worried attempts by museum librarians to classify it – by turning these efforts into something else. (In the Victoria and Albert Museum, for example, twenty or thirty of the smaller items – some are only three inches square – have been put into an envelope bearing the imprint 'On Her Majesty's Service'. One assumes at first that it refers either to the Bride or to that queen in one of Duchamp's pictures, but the envelope is only a well-meaning but bureaucratic intruder.)
Typographica 2 December 1960

Hamilton's typographic version of *The Green Box* of Duchamp. I went to the Victoria and Albert Museum library to study its copy of the *Box*. There I encountered again the dichotomy of bureaucratic discipline and the laws of chance. The small loose paper fragments of Duchamp's *Box* had been put into an envelope with the imprint 'On Her Majesty's Service'.[2]

In the drawing class at Stonyhurst College an elderly art master had taught us drawing according to certain rules which I can barely remember; then Bert Lupton replaced him and in teaching me to use watercolours, he gave me a good piece of advice, saying 'put it on and leave it'; I still try to respect this element of chance when I use that medium. During the holidays in 1929 I visited an exhibition of Japanese handicrafts at the Bluecoat Galleries in Liverpool and saw the pottery of Shoji Hamada, together with other examples of Japanese handicrafts; I also bought a copy of the book or review *Kogei*, dedicated to the folkcraft movement in Japan, which had a text by Soetsu Yanagi. I can also remember some of my lamentable attempts at making and printing woodcuts according to the Japanese method. Many years later I saw the large *hanga* prints of Shiko Munakata and tried once again.

When I left Stonyhurst in 1930 I was not happy. I went to drawing classes at the Liverpool School of Art but could not imagine a working environment of which I might become a part. At that time the term 'graphic designer' did not have any meaning and even the word 'design' meant nothing in the milieu of foreign consular officials and their families. However I did discover how well-integrated the Liverpool Jewish community was, when I got to know Abraham Newman who was a student at the Liverpool School of Art; he was a disciple of Epstein. I also remember Isaac Goller who wrote plays in Yiddish and published them under the imprint of the 'Ghetto Press'. I suppose I had an acute sense of being uprooted. Shortly before my father became Chargé d'Affaires at the Ecuadorian Legation in London, I visited another exhibition at the Bluecoat Galleries, of work by the students of Professor Riley at the Liverpool University School of Architecture. This helped me to make a decision and when we moved to London I enrolled as a student at the Bartlett School of

Woodcut by Shiko Munakata 1945

Eisenstein: *The Battleship Potemkin*

Jean Renoir: *La Fille de l'Eau*

Cavalcanti: *Rien que les heures*

Architecture at University College which also gave me the opportunity to go to life classes at the Slade.

From 1933 until 1937, when my father retired from the diplomatic service, I visited Paris frequently. I had met Dido Freire again when she came to London with Catherine Hessling and the Josephine Baker Company. Dido[3] was one of three daughters of Julia Freire, widow of the late Dario Freire, Consul of Brazil in Liverpool. Catherine had been a model for Auguste Renoir, had married Jean Renoir in 1919 and had been a 'star' in his early films of the 1920s; *La Fille de l'Eau* (1924), *Nana* (1926) and *La Petite Marchande d'Allumettes* (1928) among others. Catherine had separated from Renoir in 1930 and apparently her film career had ended; she was now a dancer. I also met her son Alain,[4] then about thirteen years old, when I visited their home in Marlotte one summer. Returning to London I brought a small painting by Auguste Renoir; Catherine wished to sell it and I was to take it to Alberto Cavalcanti. He had come to work with the G.P.O. documentary film unit in 1934; his experience in sound recording was rare at that time. Nevertheless I had seen very little of the work of Renoir and Cavalcanti[5] in the avant garde silent phase of French cinema; I was more familiar with Russian or even German cinema (Murnau and Fritz Lang). I regularly went to see the Soviet films screened in that cinema under Charing Cross station, the screen shuddering slightly as the trains got up steam overhead. I believe Cavalcanti made a valuable contribution to the

3. Dido Freire, a niece of Cavalcanti, was scriptgirl for the film *La Règle du Jeu* of Renoir in 1939; they were married in 1944 in the U.S.A.
4. Alain Renoir, after joining the French forces was trained in California and served as an artillery captain in the U.S. forces in the Pacific. He is now Professor of Medieval Literature at Berkeley, California.
5. Cavalcanti's *Rien que les heures* (1926).
6. Leo Desyllas was the arch-heretic from the academic point of view at the Bartlett.

Unfinished timber church
Posorja, Ecuador

Approaching the island of
Puná, Guayas River

cinema in England; *Dead of Night* (1945), for example. At the Bartlett, certainly during my first two years I would rather have worked at, or learned a technique in the cinema than in an architect's office; I began to understand that making a film meant team work, that film had its own language.

Our year at the Bartlett was rather turbulent; some of us had read *Vers une Architecture* of Le Corbusier. Two of the heretics,[6] went to complete their training at the Architectural Association. I went to work for a short period with Robert Gardner-Medwin.

In the summer of 1937 I left England with my family; we embarked from Marseilles for Ecuador. In Guayaquil I encountered the most generous and friendly people one could hope to meet (I met them again in 1970 when I was returning from lecturing at the Universidad Católica of Valparaiso). I love the *Guayaquileños*; they have a great sense of humour and they are charming and hospitable. However the news from Europe was disturbing and I found it difficult to adapt myself to the equatorial climate.

At the Bartlett there were two of us with the same surname, though unrelated, known as 'white Wright' and 'black Wright'. When 'black Wright' was already a sick man Lance (white) Wright arrived in Guayaquil in 1938 and made some journeys into the Andean region of Ecuador until reaching Imbabura in the north, he descended towards the tropical coast of Esmeraldas, on foot most of the way, with a pair of guides cutting a path through the jungle with their machetes; that was a brave thing to do. On his return to England he joined the Merchant Marine.

My father died in 1939; my mother, my brother and I sold everything and we sailed for Valparaiso. For a time I worked in a large and fashionable architect's office in Santiago, later in Concepción. My mother died in 1942; my brother and I became 'British Latin-American Volunteers', were given British passports and embarked from Buenos Aires in the 'Morton Bay' with another contingent of Polish Latin-Americans; the 'Graf Spee' scuttled, could still be seen above the surface of the water. On arrival in England I joined the Royal Engineers, and my brother joined the Royal Armoured Corps.

Canoe and balsawood raft,
Guayas River

At the end of the war I learnt the rudiments of book typography from George Adams, while working as his assistant. George Teltscher-Adams had been a student at the Weimar Bauhaus; I am grateful for the lessons he gave me. When I was still in training in the Engineers, I met Robert Gardner-Medwin again (he was a Major in a Camouflage unit) and he introduced me to Molly Izzard, who was a FANY driver in the army. In the spring of 1946 she put me in touch with a newly formed documentary film unit known as 'Metro-News' (part of M.G.M.) in which she had become the European news editor. I was given the task of designing titles and animated visual aids (for which I improvised some techniques using a compressed air cylinder and running the film in reverse). Then I was sent to Paris to do similar work for the French language 'Metro-Journal'. But this type of cinematic journalism or documentary news feature was already becoming obsolete with the arrival of television. The cinema now had to undergo a harsh and cynical phase in its history; the era of the Cold War.

St John's Wood and the Anglo-French

Even before the Blitz there were crumbling empty houses in St John's Wood. In 1943 I arrived there, discharged medically unfit for service in the Royal Engineers. I met Kitty Stroud, whom I married later. She looked after me until eventually, I was fit enough to be trained by S.O.E. (Special Operations Executive) in decoding ciphers; they sent me to Gibraltar and I returned again before D-day.

Breakfast in St John's Wood 1945

After the war on my return from the documentary newsreel job in Paris, with Metro-Journal, Kitty took me to the old St John's Wood art school to meet Alfred Rozelaar Green. He was transforming the art school into a cultural centre and 'free academy'; this was an attempt to give St John's Wood something after the pattern of the Académie de la Grande Chaumière in Montparnasse. It was called 'the Anglo-French Art Centre' and Eduardo Paolozzi called it 'the Anglo-Art French Centre'. Alf Green invited many celebrities to lecture or to give studio tutorials for brief periods or for a term. They included Oscar Dominguez, Fernand Léger, André

May 15th	Inauguration of the opening of the Centre. Private View—Paintings by André Lhote.
May 16th	Opening of the Art School.
May 23rd	Lecture by André Lhote—"La peinture en trois personnes."
June 5th	Private View—Paintings by Bernard Lorjou.
June 13th	Violin Recital—Devy Erlih and Ernest Lush.
June 20th	Lecture by Fernand Leger (Prof. Denis Saurat in the chair)—"Impressions d'Amérique."
July 3rd	Private View—Paintings by Fred Klein.
July 4th	Lecture by l'Abbé Morel (Herbert Read in the chair)—"Picasso."
August 3rd	Private View—Paintings by Vincent Guignebert and Jacques Lagrange.
September 3rd	Private View—Tapestries by Jean Lurçat.
September 25th	Lecture by Tristan Tzara (Miss Todd in the chair)—"Surréalisme et l'après guerre."
September 30th	Lecture by Jean Lurçat (Robin Ironside in the chair)—"La Tapisserie."
October 3rd	Private View—Paintings by François Desnoyer.
October 10th	Lecture by Jean Cassou (Robin Ironside in the chair)—"La Peinture moderne et l'humanisme."
November 8th	Private View—English Painters.

Jankel Adler	Hubert
Francis Bacon	Robert MacBryde
Robert Colquhoun	Julian Trevelyan

The exhibition was opened by M. Varin (French Cultural Relations) and Mr. Philip James (Arts Council of Great Britain).

This exhibition will be sent to Paris in June at the Galerie de France.

November 18th	Concert of Eastern Music on behalf of the Indian Famine Relief Committee.
December 6th	The Café is opened. Dance. Formation of a members' and students' Committee.
December 6th	Opening of an exhibition of members' and students' works.

Part of a programme from the Anglo-French Art Centre 1946

Lhote, Tristan Tzara and others. There was an etching press with which Roger Lacourière demonstrated and directed a printmaking workshop. Our friend Leslie Curtis was engaged as a tutor in the painting studio at the Anglo-French; he had been persuaded by Molly Izzard to come to St. John's Wood from Dublin. Jankel Adler also came to the Anglo-French with Colquhoun and MacBryde, and Leslie's paintings were influenced by the poetic linear style of Jankel Adler. Kitty also told me about Anthony Froshaug and his Albion press, on which he was printing some programmes for Alf Green. Froshaug's unique concept and practice of typography were a lesson for me. The euphoric post-war phenomenon of the Anglo-French could not really survive as an art school. Pupils enrolled now depended upon grants from an Education Authority, which in turn required an identifiable and structured pedagogic programme from the art school. The Anglo-French was really a club in a woody London backwater, in which the neighbours did not relish noisy festivities on such occasions as the Quatorze Juillet.

The ICA in Dover Street

In December 1950 the Institute of Contemporary Arts was opened in Dover Street. The following year Richard Hamilton mounted 'Growth and Form' which he had devised as an exhibition. Although many of the subjects presented as large photographic 'blow-ups' are to be found as illustrations in the two volumes of D'Arcy Thompson's book, Richard Hamilton did further research in the Science and Natural History Museum archives so as to select such images as zoological microphotos or high speed instantaneous pictures (up to one fifty-thousandth of a second), for his exhibition. Other exhibitions of a similar pattern were to follow, including 'Parallel of Life and Art' devised by Nigel Henderson, Eduardo Paolozzi and Alison and Peter Smithson in 1953, and 'Man Machine and Motion' by Richard Hamilton in 1955. These exhibits had a pedagogic value and discussions were usually arranged between a platform of speakers and the audience for the topic. Eventually some of the speakers developed into talented and witty performers, as occurred with Peter Reyner Banham and Cedric Price. There were also lively performers who devised Happenings such as Gustav Metzger, who had been a student at the Anglo-French. In the early days in Dover Street the photographer Richard Lannoy was the curator of the ICA gallery and he helped to bring together the people who later were known as the 'Independent Group'; they included Alloway, Reyner Banham, Hamilton, McHale, Paolozzi, Del Renzio and the Smithsons. The IG started their discussions in 1952 on such topics as modern technology and its emblems, automobile design and domestic gadgets (which were still pretty scarce in England at that time, as were the glossy magazines in which they were advertised).

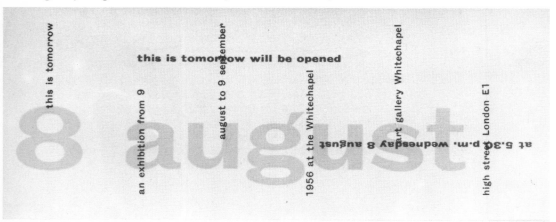

The Central School of Arts and Crafts

In 1952 the Central School of Arts and Crafts began to include some part-time or evening classes of an experimental nature. Nigel Henderson had a class working on photographic processing of images and experiments in photographic techniques. In the department of textile design, Eduardo Paolozzi began to demonstrate his use of collage technique with ready-made elements in printed surface design. Anthony Froshaug now came to redefine the teaching of typography in the graphic design department which, under Jesse Collins, was still known as the department of book production. Froshaug gave me the idea and opportunity to try out what Lawrence Gowing has aptly called 'extempore typography'. The method was to arrive at a design or typographic statement by moving printing units around on the bed of an Albion press, while making a series of impressions from wood letter and other type-high printing units. Ken Garland, who was a student then, produced some remarkable results in this way. The work, on the whole, was rather in the spirit of H. N. Werkman, the Dutch painter and printer. As Theo Crosby has put it, we had '. . . a cell of part-time students and supporters', since some of my friends even joined the class to keep up the required quota of attendance for the class to continue. The 'loyal supporters' included Pat Crooke, Germano Facetti, Bernard Myers and Joseph Rykwert. When I met Theo Crosby, who was then Technical Editor of the magazine, *Architectural Design*, he gave me the task of designing the interior and exterior of a stand (a timber cube) which he had designed for the Building Exhibition at Olympia. This was, in a way, a landmark for me because I discovered something which I was able to carry out on a much larger scale when I worked with Theo on the Exhibition and Congress buildings on the South Bank in 1961, for the VI International Architectural Congress in London. By 1956 the 'cell' at the Central School had folded, however I worked with Theo Crosby on the exhibition at the Whitechapel Gallery 'This is Tomorrow'.

H. N. Werkman, from *The Next Call*

Exhibition stand for Standard Catalogue Company and *Architectural Design* at the Building Exhibition, London 1955 by Theo Crosby and Edward Wright

Kitty and a wrecked motor car in Notting Hill Gate (1963). When we moved to Notting Hill Gate in the early sixties, we also encountered ethnic food, Black Consciousness and Concrete poetry in the neighbourhood. *Photograph by Stella Snead*

The end of the fifties

I was now finding it difficult to make a living and Kitty encouraged me to accept a job in a technical advertising agency as a designer and copywriter; I don't regret the experience but it was most depressing while it lasted. There I met Edwin Taylor, fresh from his design studies at the Central School and he more or less became my assistant until we both moved to another advertising agency where Henrion was the art director, at that time. Edwin and I worked as a team on the design of advertisements for Decca records.

In 1956 I went to the Royal College of Art, tutoring the first year in the school of graphic design. In the following year, Germano Facetti told me that a team was being set up, to enable Bertrand Russell to bring out an illustrated history of western philosophy, at Rathbone Books where Germano and Edwin were working as art editors. Eventually I left the RCA to join the team as the designer, with Paul Foulkes who looked after the text of this book.

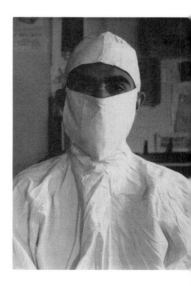

An art editor testing an image. Edwin Taylor at Rathbone Books, disguised as a surgeon.

The Painter as Designer   *Theo Crosby*

Edward Wright is a curious tom-cat creature, ambivalent, wayward, solitary, compounded of purrs and claws. I first met him in 1953, but had had for many years pinned on my bed-sit wall the card from his Mayor Gallery show in 1948. It was a marvellous drawing of a gas burner. It had a quality and an energy which I recognised at once, and cherished.

When I became assistant editor to Monica Pidgeon on *Architectural Design,* I was expected to layout the pages of the magazine. It didn't seem very difficult, but I was acutely conscious that I really needed some instruction. I was rebuffed at the Central School where I went to ask advice, but after a while heard of the evening class that Edward Wright was teaching there. I was too busy doing sculpture in the evenings so I didn't join but I saw some of the products, and met some of the students: Germano Facetti, Pat Crooke . . . and was drawn a little into Edward's circle of friends. After a while I was able to design the stand for *Architectural Design* at the Building Exhibition and Edward Wright produced the overlaid graphic decorations. It was a model collaboration, easy and so professional.

At this time, about 1955, we managed to insert Edward into the Whitefriars Press[1] as art director. We worked quite closely together and I finally received some instruction in magazine layout, and am very grateful. He is a born teacher with that elusive knack of instructing without making it painful or overbearing. His own enthusiasms – for example for Werkman or Sandberg, for the shape of letters, for the feel of tools and implements worn by use – were infectious. And all the more powerful because the enthusiasm was innocent, without guile or affectation.

We were involved also in the 'This is Tomorrow' exhibition at the Whitechapel Gallery in 1956. I sold the ads and Edward designed and produced the catalogue. It's an amusing document, full of earnest young men now pillars of the establishment. The show was organised on the principle that each group did what it liked, produced its own catalogue material, its own poster. These all used Edward Wright's logotype to unify the images, but it was my first experience at a loose, horizontal organisation of equals. We have

1. Part of the Standard Catalogue Co, the owners of *Architectural Design.*

brought it, nearly 30 years later to a kind of practical and efficient reality at Pentagram.

Edward Wright was here a most feline exemplar: willing collaborator, but quite independent. Separate with a dry intelligence, but always something positive and professional.

'This is Tomorrow' was a success which seemed even more successful later on to those too young to visit. It gave us all a little confidence and we were involved in several small shows soon after. Edward moved over to teach at the Royal College of Art in 1958. In the next year he had a show at the Mayor Gallery, and we brought out an issue of *Uppercase* to celebrate it. This little magazine, which had been largely inspired by Edward, was published in a tiny edition of 1000 by Whitefriars Press, and given away half to the Press's customers and another 500 to friends of *Architectural Design*. It very soon became a rare book. This show, innocent, earnest and unpretentious and full of good things was savaged in a review by Lawrence Alloway and I think Edward was very much upset, and taken aback. He turned to teaching more definitively, though could still be persuaded to a collaboration.

Our next enterprise was the International Union of Architects Congress on the South Bank in 1961. I had stumbled on the job and through the generosity of Sir Robert Matthew it grew into two temporary buildings on the site of the 1951 Festival's Dome of Discovery. It was an opportunity to put some Art in Architecture theory into practice. The exhibition building contained some existing sculptures by Paolozzi, Kneale, Turnbull, Adams, Brian Wall and myself, and specially made works by Bernard Cohen, Hamilton, McHale, Wise, Stroud and Plumb. In the central area Tony Caro showed his first abstract work.

The Headquarters building was a much tighter collaboration, in which the building surfaces were worked directly. William Turnbull created colour walls in most of the rooms; John Ernest made a remarkable wall in the Press Room; Mary Martin and Anthony Hill made large wall constructions in the main concourse, with mobiles by Kenneth Martin.

Exterior view of stand at Building Exhibition 1958

Briefing a signwriter on the South Bank site of the IUA congress 1961

End view of Exhibition
building of IUA congress,
London 1961

Edward Wright made the titling panels, and also
designed the huge graphic wall to the exhibition
building, one of his most felicitous works. He also
designed all the graphics and signing, including John
Ernest's 60ft high scaffold tower, and the banners that
enclosed the central space. It was all marvellously
bright, cheerful and intelligent, and was well received.
I remember we all felt very pleased with each other and
have I suppose often wondered why such occasions,
generous and spontaneous are so rare. It was however
for me to herald a change of direction, for shortly
afterwards I went to work in Euston Station and put
graphics and publishing temporarily behind me.
Edward Wright, too, moved on, to Chelsea and we saw
each other much less. Our last collaboration was his
section of the British Design show in the Musée des
Arts Decoratifs in 1969.

Edward Wright always seemed to be a kind of exemplar
of the artist, of his difficulties, and of his strategies.
An artist spends much of his life simply getting started,
needing money, needing patrons and work. Survival is
always in doubt. The work, always done in private is
thrust into the public domain and its reception is often
hostile or indifferent. Wright's strategy of privacy and
defensiveness about his paintings was matched by his
openness as a teacher and graphic designer. Yet it was,
of course, the work as a painter that made the designer
so thoroughly, intelligently original; and the shyness
that made it possible to teach with such delicacy and
understanding.

Lettering for *house of the future* at Olympia, London 1956.

Architects: Alison and Peter Smithson

This alphabet was also used for
a *Horizon* television title
designed by Bernard Lodge

abcd

efghij

klmno

pqrst

uvwx

yz

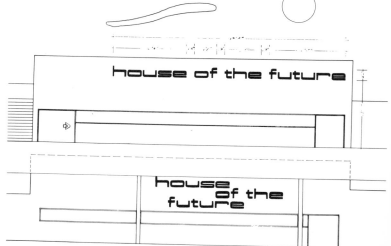

house of the future

house of the
future

Alphabet for a study in legibility 1963

ABCDE
FGHIJK
LMNOP
QRSTU
VWXYZ
1234567890

Lettering for Hinsley House, King Street, Covent Garden 1964

Architects: Bellalta, Hattrell and Lance Wright

ABCDEFG
HIJKLM
NOPQRS
TUVWX
YZ 123
4567890

Foundation stone for Churchill College, Cambridge 1961

Architects: Richard Sheppard, Robson and Partners

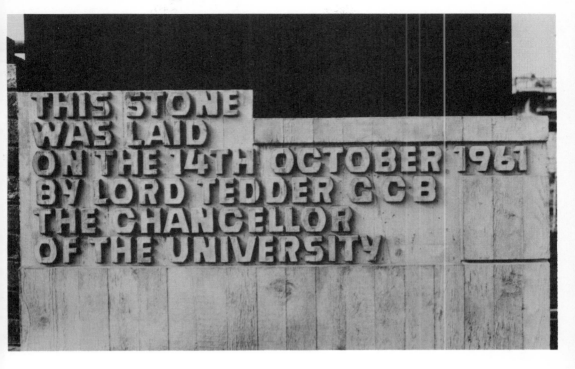

The Churchill College
foundation stone is a piece of
black slate. The inscription is
cast in concrete. A lighter form
of this lettering is cast in
bronze, at Imperial College,
London.

photograph by Alan Bartram

Bronze plaque for Imperial College, London 1963

Rotating sign for New Scotland Yard 1968

Architects: Chapman, Taylor and Partners

ABCDEFG
HIJKLMN
OPQRST
UVWXY
Z 1234
567890

0123
4567
89G

Numerals for internal door signing have a slightly heavier proportion.

photographs by Euan Duff

Teaching and experiment   *Ken Garland*

Yes, well I suppose I know quite a lot more about
Futurism, and Dada, and Constructivism, and all that,
than I did when I was frolicking with large hunks of
type matter on the hand press in Edward Wright's
evening class at the Central in 1952/53. Now I can tell
you the date of Marinetti's *Zang tumb tuum* and the date
of the first issue of *Lacerba* and Hugo Ball's sound poem
Karawane and Picabia's cover for *Le coeur à barbe*
and Lissitzky's *Tale of two squares* – go on, ask me.
Godammit, though, even the students of my ex-students
know all that stuff nowadays, don't they?

But I'd swap all these historicisms for another good
bash at the old platen right *now,* with a merciful
mindblank about what those geysers did before we got
onto the scene. See, Edward didn't go on about them at
all, though he knew all about them, of course. No, he
just set up the conditions for us to have fun, and
feelings, and excitement, and the belief that we were
inventing all the time. No, that wasn't a confidence
trick: it was a fruitful and considerate teaching method,
and speaking for myself, it has supplied me with a head
of steam that's kept me going for 30 years. There are
still some things I started on then that I'm waiting to
develop tomorrow, or maybe the day after, and the hell
with nostalgia.

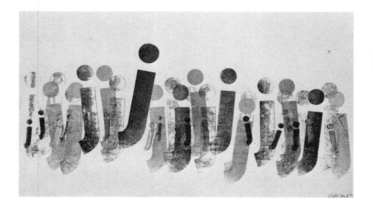

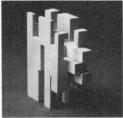

Mark Lintell *Magdalene*

The interlocking kit *EW*

During my part-time teaching at Cambridge University School of Architecture I had thought about a problem dealing with the joint, and with Colin St John Wilson had prepared a task for first year students. Two similar volumes were to be closed and locked in a required number of positions, of which the first would give a clue to the other variations. The following year the brief was revised and given clearer *formal* definition by Peter Eisenman at Cambridge and another interpretation was given to the first year students at the Architectural Association by Tony Eardley; this gave us the pretext to arrange a visit and an exchange of ideas between students and teaching staff of the two schools.

Architectural Association Journal 1963

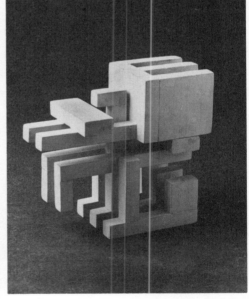

Michael Driver *Christ's*

Piers Pendred *Trinity Hall*

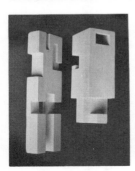

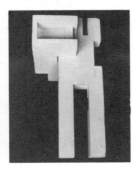

From a *to* z

This foundation course project was given at Chelsea School of Art in 1967. The typographic designs were required to show the relative frequence of different letters in English usage.[1] It was also an exercise in letterpress composition.

Three designs by foundation course students.

1. 'Now, in English, the letter which most frequently occurs is *e*. Afterwards, the succession runs thus: *aoidhnrstuycfglmwbkpqxz.*' Edgar Allan Poe *The Gold-Bug.*

Hunters running. Rock
painting from Castellón de
la Plana

Writing is a technique of visual communication. Marks
that were made on a surface were originally ritualistic
rather than descriptive. One can think of the paintings
on the walls of caves as an early unsystematic
foreshadowing of writing. Fine art as we know it did
not then exist.

True writing begins with the pictogram which is a sign
typifying something seen, having its particular meaning
and legible to those who are familiar with this sign and
the system of notation to which it belongs. But
pictograms by their nature are not suited to
representing qualities and abstract ideas in isolation;
and as things and qualities become distinguished from
each other in people's minds the next, or ideographic,
stage in writing occurs.

The phonogram stage is the third, when a sign is used
to represent a sound, and this change is marked less by
formal simplification in the beginning than by a new
function. Characters in the Chinese script are
ideographic, whereas similar characters in Japanese are
used phonetically. With the phonetic stage one reaches
the alphabet and here the pictographic origins of the
letters are eventually forgotten. In the Chinese script
the split between thought (idea) and feeling (shape) does
not occur; calligraphy is practised in China with a
vitality unknown in the West. It has always been
considered of far greater importance than painting,
which derives from it.

Formal simplification in writing is induced by the need
to save time, and time has a parallel effect upon the
choice of vehicle or support which carries the message.
In terms of time, there can be two types of message,
namely the one which has an immediate and the one
which has a cumulative effect upon the human target.
This grouping results from one fact alone. The target
can either stop and read the message or he can carry it
away in his pocket to learn and inwardly digest later on.
In the first group the message is localized and becomes a
part of its habitat; it is public. Dimensionally, sky-
writing is an extreme example from this group,
although it is very ephemeral. The second group
includes things such as books in a convenient format to
be held on one's hand. Every rule is upheld by its

exception and the great borderline case between the two groups is, of course, the newspaper. It is displayed and forms a part of its environment, then it becomes the property of a reader who may read it and leave it somewhere; but its life is probably not finished yet. It is used to protect someone from the unexpected shower of rain, to cut out paper patterns, to wrap up fish and chips, to light a fire. The newspaper is so ubiquitous, so protean that it could be the machine's equivalent of something organic like an animal's hide. Localized writing reveals publicly the growth, the change and the decay of its environment, and for this reason the newspaper should be included in this group rather than in the other.

Writing forms in antiquity evolved to the same extent on a building surface as they did on the surface of a prepared writing material. The clay brick was a writing material for cuneiform. This method of inscribing pictograms on wet clay with a sharpened reed was probably composed before 3000 B.C. by the Sumerians. They used cuneiform to record calculations, ritual or contracts which were sometimes baked inside another wall of clay. The bond would be hidden until the outer crust was broken. In time the characters were simplified, stylized and became ideograms when they were used to record the despotic triumphs of the Assyrians who used cuneiform on stone. This incised writing on massive walls appears at times to be a compact horizontal texture which penetrates the low relief of vertical processional figures. One can see two methods of recording at right angles to each other and almost in opposition, the one public, the other private. The low relief figuration is a narrative, the cuneiform is a system for filing events. The palace walls at Nimrud were its archives, to be read by rulers, priests or scribes.

In Greece and Rome writing became public, slaves could read. On the columns of Trajan and Marcus Aurelius the recording of iconographic processes are integrated. The inscription on the base is ritualistic and the spiral reliefs are a narrative, a kind of writing. The processes are fused into the column, the focal point of a Roman environment. The social context determines the extent to which writing can become a part of its environment, or break into it as a protest, or flourish as

Glyptic: cuneiform inscription on bas-relief from Nimrud
British Museum

62

Calligraphic: rue Visconti
Paris 1955

Tectonic: Boulevard St Germain
Paris 1955

a parasitic growth. It is technique which determines character or style. All writing (with the exception of printing which is its diffusion through mechanical reproductive processes) can be considered in technical terms, as glyptic, calligraphic or tectonic. *Glyptic* writing is formed in its support by incising, moulding, pressing or repoussé techniques. *Calligraphic* writing is drawn or painted over its support. Graffiti are sometimes a hybrid of these two categories. *Tectonic* writing appears to be a nineteenth century invention. It is writing composed from letters which are independent structural units attached to a support or more typically attached to an almost invisible frame which allows the letters to be suspended over the façade. Writing reflects its environment not only in the form and style of letters, but more profoundly in the technical process used to make them an integral part of their surroundings. Often the first appearance of a message gives the clue to some social tension or process of transformation no more obvious than the collection of little cards pinned and taped onto the budding door bells of a still respectable mansion. When letters become separate structural units, they can be made of any material including electric light bulbs and neon tube. With this technique writing invades the environment until a surprising symbiosis is reached. The environment built out of visual communications. Times Square and Piccadilly Circus become heaven to those who can't read and at least a playground for those who can.

The easel picture according to Panofsky is a 'man-made object demanding to be experienced aesthetically'. In other words it is an object which requires intuition and an attitude of mental re-creation on the part of the spectator. The man who makes this object is known as a painter, although he may not use paint always nor even use it at all. His picture may consist of ready-made coloured substances glued together; it may include a whole magpie's nest of relics from other crafts and industries whenever technique is used as a creative process. If it is a painting one expects it to look like paint or like sand, feathers or sacking if they are the real physical ingredients. At times when an unobtrusive film of paint represented the window into which the spectator looked, the technique could be self-effacing and smooth (Van Eyck, Piero della Francesca, David).[1]

So the physical ingredients of a painting only turn it into an image because the painter intended it to be that thing. And who is the painter? He is, to begin with, a maker of images and his identity is always modified by exterior and interior forces, by the time and the society to which he belongs, by his faith and doubts, by his material limitations, and finally by the accumulating evidence of the works which he produces. A creative process includes both 'task' and 'play', and the 'play' element is also revealed in the *persona* which the painter acquires. Picasso, for example, is technically so brilliant and so articulate in inventing and handling visual symbols that he becomes the archparodist and transformer of his predecessors' themes; giving us surprising variations and comments on the works of Cranach, El Greco, Poussin, Delacroix, Courbet, and many others. Many writers about pre-history agree that the image-maker of the late palaeolithic or ice-age was the priest or magician of his social group.[2]

Prehistoric men believed in a mystic identity between human being and animal; this belief was celebrated in a ritual play performed by the magician, disguised in animal form. This also shows that from earliest times painting had been used to depict simultaneous aspects of one being and the idea that a single person can have more than one nature. The painter participated in the ritual when he made his images of it. Kühn even suggests that both priest and painter may have been the

1. Panofsky also says: 'Where the sphere of practical objects end, and that of "art" begins, depends, then, on the "intention" of the creators. This "intention" cannot be absolutely determined. In the first place, "intentions" are . . . incapable of being defined with scientific precision. In the second place, the "intentions" of those who produce objects are conditioned by the standards of their period and environment.'
Erwin Panofsky: *Meaning in the Visual Arts.*

2. Kühn, describing a painting in the cavern of the Trois Frères says: 'Above them all is the picture of the magician himself, the portrait of the man who may, indeed, have executed some of the engravings. With his large, dark eyes he gazes at the visitor. This shaman wears upon his head the mask of a stag with its antlers. Bear's paws cover his hands and a horse's tail hangs from his waist. One leg is raised as in a dance.'
Herbert Kühn: *Rock Pictures of Europe.*

Wizard playing a flute in the cavern of Les Trois Frères.

3. The concept of play merges quite naturally with that of holiness. Any prelude of Bach, any line of tragedy proves it. By considering the whole sphere of so-called primitive culture as a play-sphere we pave the way to a more direct and more general understanding of its peculiarities than any meticulous psychological or sociological analysis would allow. Primitive or, let us say, archaic ritual is thus sacred play, indispensable for the well-being of the community, full of cosmic insight and social development but always play in the sense Plato gave to it – an action accomplishing itself outside and above the necessities and seriousness of everyday life. In this sphere of sacred play the child and the poet are at home with the savage.
Johan Huizinga: *Homo Ludens*.

same person. A relationship between ritual and play in primitive society has also been suggested in *Homo Ludens* by Johan Huizinga: 'In play as we conceive it the distinction between belief and make-believe breaks down'.[3]

Task

Poetry is saturated with the play instinct and at the same time the poet has a task. Now according to Mallarmé the task of the poet is 'to purify the language of the tribe'. We, through fumbling confusion of thought or evasion of reality, devalue and deaden our words. The poet recreates them and in a spirit of play gives them back to us. Something similar can occur with images when they are used as visual symbols to embody ideas. We are now verbal and visual symbol consumers. The painter is still an image maker but as a visual symbol creator he has been outpaced by graphic artists, anonymous package designers, film directors, and advertising men. In a way the easel painter is still the image-maker of the tribe, but what he makes is now reduced and altered on the moving belt of mass-symbol production. Hundreds of thousands of people may enjoy good coloured postcard reproductions of modern paintings; millions more may enjoy less faithful reproductions in the mass-circulation weeklies. The graphic artist, the designer, and the ad-man are influenced by the easel painter on a stylistic level, and the easel painter is influenced by their day-to-day choice of symbols.

During the ice-age task and play were sacred. The task included a given theme, site, and materials. The interpretation of the theme, the use of materials, and above all the use of the site, were vitalized by the instinct of play. Nowadays the painter is not given a theme nor is he asked to create visual symbols for his society. In spite of this the will to make images survives.

Play

In an oblique way people are still ready to look at new images and become captivated by them. The painter is now his own taskmaster and his *persona* has acquired surprising traces of the surgeon, the explorer and the cook. The Italian painter Burri probably considers his materials from a rather surgeonlike point of view. This is illustrated by an extract from the article 'Burri Makes a Picture' in the American magazine *Art News:* 'The plastic blobs on the protuberances had become tacky and it was time to proceed to their *slabbramento,* a term often used in the sense of "opening a wound". With a palette knife incisions were made in the blobs along the curving ridge of the swellings, and the edges of the plastic were retracted and secured with straight pins (later removed)'. Such disguises are usually a part of the painter's creative play misinterpreted by self-conscious observers as an attempt to evade their critical pigeon-holing. The painter's play develops with his time and environment, but many 'art lovers' cling to devalued attitudes. One uses certain faculties to absorb a painting, faculties which are made poorer if they are not used every day on the things which surround us. Domestic appliances, advertisements, and people's everyday gestures need not be placed in a caste system below that which includes sculptures, easel pictures, and mime. We can't withhold feelings for rare occasions and at the same time keep them alive. But many people think it necessary to have a special attitude in front of a fine-art object. A special attitude which is usually induced by a device such as an elaborate picture-frame. This attitude is now vestigial, a remnant out of a vast wardrobe of gestures belonging to the days when people wore wigs. In fact, as Huizinga points out, the practice of framing pictures in a certain way was contemporaneous with the vogue for wigs in the seventeenth century. The frame is used to isolate the picture and pay homage to it as the wig frames the face and makes it appear nobler. It is very easy to detect the shrine-creating impulse at work in people's houses, and the 'pin-up' is just another proof of our need for images. The appearance of elaborate frames and glass cases implies that the impulse has lost touch with reality and a 'special attitude' is being fabricated. A curious example is the stuffed fish in a glass case. What could be more natural than to go fishing, catch something, and have a record of one's catch? It is equally natural to eat what one has caught, and photography might appear the obvious means of recording one's catch. But this is not enough from the angler's point of view, as a photograph is not the same as a trophy. So some people prefer to embalm the fish in a glass case rather than eat it. They are even ready to spend several hours cleaning

Gyo-Taku
The inscription reads:
The place where he caught the
fish, called Wada Bo-ha tei
300 copies 8. viii. 1943
by Kino-Shita

it, to let six weeks elapse while it dries, to spend another week mounting it, and finally to devote a great deal of time, labour and expense to try to make the embalmed fish look alive in its cumbersome glass case. A primitive impulse is concealed in a clumsy nineteenth-century illusionistic technique very much in sympathy with repository art. The extraordinary thing about the stuffed fish in a glass case is that the embalming and model-making techniques destroy all one's awareness of the fish's real nature and of the moment when it was snatched out of its element and died. The remnants are there but utterly disguised by the illusionistic faking. Japanese fishermen have their own way of making trophies. Known as *Gyo-Taku*, it consists of rubbing the catch with India ink and taking an impression before the ink dries. You can have your fish and eat it. The fish goes to the kitchen and a brief, tactile and lively image remains to be contemplated. Usually it is very difficult to see the complete transition from an idea through creative technique to the end-product of the process, the image, although it is becoming less difficult and less unusual than before. The image in the process of becoming is illustrated in another example from Japan, on the lid of a writing box by Shunshō. It represents a woman squirting black toothstain from her mouth on to a screen and writing the characters *Koi-wo-shinobu* or 'perseverence in love'. One sees how the ideogram on the screen has assumed a particular form as a result of this painterly game with the toothstain straight from the woman's mouth. Idea and form, thought and feeling are joined in a calligraphy which uses no hand or instrument. This is creative technique at play and the image is found within the unusual limitations. A painter learns to be economical like a farmer, like a cook, and his equipment influences his development, impels him to work by arousing senses of smell and touch. The tubes and tins of colours, the bottles and containers of turpentine, oil, and varnish, the dry crusts of paint, the brushes, knives, and rags are a physical part of his environment, completed by the presence of the work in progress. This accumulated work is also a witness to be accepted or denounced. It is capable of crowding him out, forcing him to react, or nauseating him and making his life unbearable unless he renews himself. Whenever a person or a group of people absorb an image or a sign, they tend to modify, increase, or devalue its content, and some painters have been unable to overcome the crisis created by their devalued accumulated work or to reconcile themselves to their own limitations. They have killed themselves. Perhaps play had stopped; it may have done so, or more probably the game had now become as some games are, one of life and death.

From the cover of a Japanese lacquer writing box by Shimsho. A method by which black tooth stain is skilfully squirted on to a screen to form a message. Style evolves to some extent according to the laws of chance.

A child artist in Rome. Inventive variations are sometimes made upon the themes given by other children on the same wall surface.

From *The Arts, Artists and Thinkers* edited by John Todd, Longmans Green & Co, 1957.

This is a shorter version of a text written to accompany a collection of photographs by Herbert Spencer, of pointing fists and arrows used for directing traffic, published in *Typographica* 1965.

Emphatic fist, informative arrow *EW*

The signboard, supported on its vertical post with the directional end shaped into a pointing fist is really the dummy of a man met at the crossroads who answers a question by extending his arm, pointing and naming a place. The pointing index finger was in the first place a gesture of command. Then, in manuscripts and in printing, it was a sign for emphasis until the nineteenth century, when its typographic use and appearance became almost ornamental. Even if it had not become so decorative, the fist did not suit the needs of mechanised transport, which demanded a sign in keeping with scientific ideas, implying speed, and adaptable to a more complex environment. Arrows can be used to indicate turns and be made to branch off each other. In a sense, the arrow had been tamed before it was used in this way and its meaning as a weapon had been forgotten with the arrival of firearms and other machines of war. It had to lose its sting in the sense given by Canetti[1], before it could be an adaptable sign. Towards the end of the nineteenth century archery had become a sport for ladies; one finds two crossed arrows with a target as carved and gilded decoration on the back of a Florentine chair in Napoleonic style in the Pitti Palace[2]. About the year 1800 arrows were being used as indicators on weathervanes in the States of Maine, Massachusetts and Pennsylvania. These carved and gilded arrows were perhaps attached to weathervanes because an arrow flies in the air, and the war arrows of the American Indians were not a threat in the eastern States by that time. However simple in detail and silhouette, the arrow on a weathervane is a representation which has been found and assembled, whereas in modern traffic situations the arrow must be an informative pointer shaped to give a phased message to a moving target approaching it from several directions. The sign on the highway is really not an arrow at all; it is a diagram which can change direction and be read from a distance at windscreen level. We can call them arrows because 'arrow' now means a certain kind of sign.

1. '... Every command consists of *momentum* and *sting*. The momentum forces the recipient to act, and to act in accordance with the content of the command; the sting remains behind in him.
... This relationship to the horse plays a decisive part in the command-economy of man, but among the Mongols there is another important factor. This is the *arrow*, the exact image of the original, non-domesticated command. An arrow is hostile; it is meant to kill. It travels straight through space.'
Elias Canetti: *Crowds and Power*
(Eng. trans. Gollancz 1960)

2. *La sedia italiana nei secoli* (ediz., centro studi Triennale nona Triennale 1951).

Paul Van Ostaijen *EW*

Paul Van Ostaijen was born in Antwerp on 22 February
1896 and died thirty-two years later of tuberculosis in
a sanatorium at Miavoye-Anthée on 17 March 1928.
Before he finished his studies at school he had begun to
write and contribute to newspapers and weeklies
around the year 1912. In the main phases of
development which followed, *Feesten van Angst en Pijn,
Bezette Stad* and *Het Eerste Boek van Schmoll*, it is easy
to recognize the changes in graphic expression due to
his uncommon visual sense of writing and typography.
A notable use of graphic means in poetry can lead to a
visual dilemma when the Flemish language confronts
the foreign reader. The pages of *Bezette Stad* provoke
random intuitive interpretations when a knowledge of
Flemish is lacking and other poems not only look too
accessible to readers who know fragments of the
language but do also suggest that a visual form was his
main attempt. Had this been the case the
cosmopolitanism of *Bezette Stad* could have led to more
extensive work in either French or German. But Van
Ostaijen chose the Flemish language and the graphic
pattern is a true notation of the sound, sense and
rhythm of his poems in that language. The pattern also
measures time, indicating pauses by typographic spaces.
Language and theme are not to be separated because
the substance with which his poems are made is speech;
the graphic form is the geometry of that sound. For
Van Ostaijen Flemish, rather than the French of
literary Antwerp, was useful as common every-day
speech favouring the irony of his spirit.

In 1921 *Bezette Stad* ('Occupied City') was published, to
the design of René Victor and Oscar Jespers. This
turbulent and spontaneous poem has 153 pages in the
original quarto edition (28cm × 21.5cm). The nine or so
distinct graphic techniques in the text are used rather
like those of a cameraman or film maker to build up a
sequence on the idea of wartime invasion and
occupation of a town. As in a film, certain thematic
devices recur and are given a new context. The text is
set in Caslon, mainly 10pt, but in other sizes as large as
48pt. Many display faces are combined with this. Linear
(technical drawing) stencils are sometimes used to
repeat and break up a word; larger stencil plates are
used as emblems. There are the woodcuts by Oscar
Jespers and the anamorphic words and phrases designed

STEMMING

Filterregen zijpel zacht
In mijn hart uw klamme klacht
En ontmacht,
Me zacht, in de nacht
Die m'in purper wacht.

Wolkenvachten,
Donkre machten,
Drijven krachten
Die versmachten
Korenkop'ren pracht.

Zijpelregen,
Zonder zegen,
Langs de wegen
Neergezegen,
Ruis in 't harte
Van de zwarte
Linden langs de laan.

Regenvlegen
Die, als narren,
Komen sarren,
Ruist nu vege
In het lege
Van mijn hart,
Moederstille smart.

Filterregen, zijpel zacht
In mijn hart uw klamme klacht.

L'Auto de la Mort from
Bezette Stad

to mark the beginning of a new part in the sequence; there are also calligraphic words stereotyped for repetition of a theme and letters and phrases built up from type borders and rules. Then there is a page of the poet's handwriting like a scrawled message on the back of a postcard. The friends who survived him and those who felt his influence may have named *Bezette Stad* as a work which identified a movement or tendency to which they belonged; afterwards it probably became a convenient label for the others who wanted to classify him neatly. This is unjust because *Bezette Stad* could be omitted and Van Ostaijen would remain a great and uncommon poet, unmistakable in his rhythmic musical language.

Bezette Stad begins with a dedication to Mister So-and-so and speaks of the dream world of the film, the mythical Fantômas of Feuillade, the Last of the Mohicans, cosmetics, the tango, the last Pernod; NIHIL is repeated, the illusion cracks. The threatened town, Bedreigde Stad, comes next, to the one, two, one, two of an approaching army; flame shells dropping and the imminent violation of the town is ironically mitigated by the doors of a brothel, *un client mesdames voyons*, the exodus and occupation by troops. Now there are abandoned forts, the lonely town, the empty docks, Holle Haven full of labelled cargo and the names of deserted ships which won't reach their destination. The Zeppelin appears, the cinema is empty, buffet, bar, barman, barmaid are all alone; this finishes with a town still life and a hand which phosphorizes the sky with

Tale

Filtering rain seeps softly in my heart your wetness echoes a moment,
tender in my night of transformed purple hope.

White cloud fleeces, dark forces driving strength powering verses
ripening corn-splendour.

Seeping rain and no net upon the way, unblessed murmuring in the
heart of the black lindens along the lane.

Flailing rain fool-like come teasing departed voices in the void
of my heart's mother-soothed pain.

Filtering rain seeps softly in my heart your wetness echoes.

Stemming Paul van Ostaijen   May 1914
translation by Michael O'Casey and Peter Mayer

Boven   in de   VIolette hemel

donker   violET

fosforesseert

GEle

HAnD

Vijf   heel   duidelike

5   VIngers

five fingers (searchlights, flares?). Dead Sunday, *Dodezondag*, follows and the town is in mourning, lips murmur a sigh, a banal dance begins and good news is faced by a poster poem, grand circus of the Holy Ghost, in the Dada spirit. The emblem, De Kringen naar Binnen is a circle turning into itself but Music Hall is an opening circle which allows the dejected round of hopelessness of the town to be broken and life can begin again. Once more the cinema is presented not as illusion but as a kinetic art of light. Asta Nielson in coloured lights; Asta, astra, *voilà*. The bar has a wardrobe full of fifty bowler hats, the town begins to dance. After the end of the closed circle comes the retreat, *de Aftocht*. Time conquers the invader, patriotic manifestations are absurd. Dada was not a formalist movement and it rejected closed tendencies, using any technique to express the Dada state of mind. From this point of view, *Bezette Stad* could be called a dadaist work.

Above in the
                    VIolet heavens
        dark   violET
phosphorizes
                    YEllow
                                HAnD
fiVe   quite distinct
        5   VIingers

Bezette Stad: In his notes Van Ostaijen points out that the capital V was also intended to neutralize the vertical symmetry at the capital I (in fingers). With regard to sound: *'Le flammand "vingers" (doigts) sera traduit en français par "ongles".'*
Het Getij April 1922.

AAN CENDRARS

Man   loopt   straat
uide stem tussen huizen
ij   roept
   klinkt klinker klaar
Blaise   Blaise   BLAI —
                      se

   gij zijt het
   Cendrars

DERDE GROTESKE

Een
    twee
een
    twee
       krachten van opgaan
       krachten van
             neergaan
de nutteloze kamp
          ons leven verbrandt
immer
immer
immer
    schoppen is troef
          nu
   harten mijnheren
        enzovoort
           enz
            z.

The last collection of poems *Het Eerste Boek van Schmoll* (1928), named after a beginner's music manual, contains poems which date back to 1920. They belong, however, to his last phase which has been called 'organic expressionism'. Organic, insofar as a process took place in which he modified spelling, inflections and participles, and eliminated punctuation, so that the text, with its spaces on the page, becomes a notation for the rhythmic sound of the poem. But it is the poem as a whole which gives the theme. The typographic structure is both visible and integral with the dynamic expression. In England the 'Imagist' poems written about this time, were allusive and show a searching use of the right noun or adjective 'to present an image'. In the structural syntax of Van Ostaijen, the verb, the word of action, matters more. In speaking of these poems Schoonhoven has said: 'In the best poems the words, their sound association and their harmonic value exist almost independently from their rational meaning. Alongside these interpretations Van Ostaijen only agrees to the internal direction of the poem itself'. In *Krities Proza II*, Van Ostaijen drew a distinction between subject and theme and in some notes on Melopée (Chant), he made this clear: '1. General movement arising from the intention to write a chant. 2. First phase – the premise – should be more positive than what follows. 3. The following phases will move increasingly into an indefinite zone and I will attempt to arrive there by pulling the premise into it more lengthily by adding a new idea or an indirect element. 4. It will probably be necessary to introduce a syncopated rhythm somewhere to give distance to what is to follow. There then is shown briefly, from its point of departure, what I would call a thematic poem . . . Now you will understand easily that without a subject matter to be put down on paper I am not tied to conventional versification; I cannot imagine at all how thematic poetry can make use of it. But even more than versification the techniques of *vers-libre* would embarrass me in that which I value most . . . The repeated rise and fall of free verse bothers me because it does not allow words to unfold in depth, to extend in duration'. 'To extend in duration' – we see the intervals in his rhythmic language as a typographical constellation.

What do you mean 'The New Avant Garde'? *EW*

Sound
The New Avant Garde sounds like an echo of *La
Nouvelle Vague*. Understandably 'the new wave' was
describing a movement in France nine years ago, in
which the sea by implication metaphorised the creative
activity of the cinema. A film is the result of an
immense collective effort, in most cases.
It is difficult to take the word avant garde very seriously
at the present time; during the last 30 years it has
become devalued to the point of becoming a cliché. To
add 'new' to this word is to make a neo-cliché in the
fashion of Son of Dracula or Bride of Frankenstein.
How about NEW new avant garde (equivalent to say
Nephew of Frankenstein)?

Interpretation
However, in art new things continue to happen,
although the process now seems to be one of osmosis,
rather than one of action and reaction. The idea of
'campaigning' in the field of art cannot be taken very
seriously when the socially dispossessed minorities, such
as urban squatters and gypsies, can show how well the
artist has become integrated into this society, in an
economical sense. Reality resides in art, which means
that a new idea, about the world or society, generates its
phenomena, even if they are not immediately legible.
The various projects for monuments by Claes
Oldenburg can now be seen as examples of revolutionary
art, or art of subversive irony.

An example
If we take as an example the Colossal monument of
Concrete Inscribed with Names of War Heroes, in the
Intersection of Canal Street and Broadway – this has
even more meaning now than in 1965. The black
humour of 500 million pounds of concrete, paralysing
traffic and blocking the view along Broadway, is helped
by the paper prepared for a class at Cornell University
by Evans, O'Brien and Schwartz to study the structural
and geological specifications. Oldenburg's work exceeds
the limit of a 'movement' label such as 'pop'.
'New avant garde' is probably an umbrella classification
covering the various experiments in art at this time.
In an urban situation in which we are confronted by the
predicament of urban squatters (and of gypsies not so
far away) it is rather difficult to believe in dangerous art
campaigning against mythical academic ramparts.

Ark Magazine No. 45 1969, edited by Alan Rickman.

This text was contributed to the 1970 International Biennale of the Poster, in Warsaw, at a symposium on *Shaping of a graphic designer's imagination*

Conversation, handwriting and the poster *EW*

Conversation

Speech operates with word and with gesture. The frequency and the volume, the changes in tone and the pauses, are in themselves non-verbal signals which shape the intended meaning of the spoken word. This vocalization is normally taken for granted, but it is in fact the gestural language of the human speech apparatus. Those instruments which allow us to survive and to enjoy life, lungs, teeth, lips and tongue, combine in a gesture to shape our words. It is not surprising that a written sign in a script should be sometimes, the recognizable pattern of the physiological gesture. The written sign itself is too deep a subject for a short paper and I would only refer to the unique psychological analysis of the origins of the alphabet by Alfred Kallir, *Sign and Design* (the psychogenetic source of the alphabet).

If in our vocalization we produce speech by an internal gesture, at the same time we use non-verbal signals which are overtly visual; bodily postures and hand and facial gestures which are continually modified as the conversation proceeds. A gestural restraint which is deliberate may be interpreted, when it is recognised, as a non-verbal signal. So in a conversation, each of the participants casts a net of words and gestures across the common situation bounded by the behaviour and experience of either one. This pattern of the process of human relationship has been schematized by R. D. Laing. This structure of communication fluctuates according to the feed-back; according to the verbal and non-verbal signals of experience which emanate from one end as a result of the verbal and non-verbal signals of behaviour at the other. Verbal communication is diachronic and in a dialogue each person is progressively conditioned by the behaviour of the other, but it is also possible to represent a particular phase in a dialogue by a synchronic schematization. The equivalent of this, in popular figurative terms, would be a 'frame' in a strip cartoon; a historical antecedent would be a detail in one of the surviving Mexican codices, in which mythical figures confront each other and speech bubbles come out from their mouths.

Speech bubble:
Figure giving instructions for weaving. (Aztec) *Codex Mendocino*, Bodleian, Oxford.

Handwriting

In handwriting the gesture is inherent. The linearity of handwriting is diachronic in its procedure, and in its

75

decoding process; however, each time that a message is handwritten, its exact meaning is qualified by the psychology and environment of the person who writes, after taking into consideration the nature of the writing equipment. This gestural nature of handwriting has probably not received the attention in England, that it has gained in other countries and in other cultures. Abstract inventions in calligraphy may require considerable anthropological unravellings, but the content can be slight. The gesture is apparent when we sign our name, write urgent messages, love letters and inspirational notes. Mechanization has, to a certain extent, embalmed calligraphy. Handwriting is read and formal lettering is merely looked at, unless there is an eloquent textural cohesion. The texture of handwriting, of lettering and of print should give a synchronic clue about the content of the message. This approximate evaluation of content can occur because handwriting, lettering and print are normally produced with a visual concept of the message as a whole; the texture and the format should then operate as calculated non-verbal signalling devices. Human speech in conversation, tends to be open-ended and sometimes unpredictable in its line of development (due to the feed-back) and the non-verbal signals are intuitive and instinctive. The textural non-verbal signal given by handwriting is an accumulated pattern of an individual human dynamism. In lettering and in print the texture results from the disposition of letters and words of a selected configuration or type. A legible text has a legible texture. We receive a signal before we start reading.

This calligraphic abstraction is an emblem used by a scribe in the Colonial period of Hispanic America. Fernando Arnedo, *Escribano Público* in the city of Guayaquil, in 1578, used it to affirm his identity and the truth of what he wrote. *Revista del Archivo Histórico del Guayas.* Edited by Julio Estrada, June 1978

The poster makes its own environment
The poster and the newspaper give continuously obliterated signals about our events and our social behaviour. Of the two, the poster was, until recently, the more public and the more popular message format; one reason being, that it was free and not for sale, the other, that it made no great demands on literacy. In some urban environments neither of the two reasons can still be considered entirely valid now. There are posters dedicated to pop-cult performers for sale in shops, and sophisticated puns are made in the text of large commercial posters. Nevertheless, the poster has to use a graphic language which is emphatic, brief and immediately understood by a human target on the

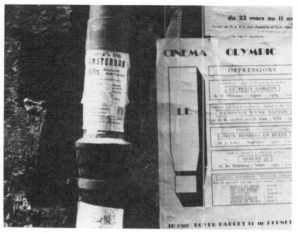

Posters on a drainpipe and a
poster tied to a tree. Both
these pictures were taken in the
neighbourhood of the Sorbonne
in Paris in 1971.

move. This human target has its attention captured by
the dynamism of the street and its message, and also the
message picked up from other posters. Among many
others, a single poster may have its meaning modified
by visually noisy neighbours or it may be aided by the
context which they give. The poster made its own
environment before the stage coach had disappeared; an
end wall of an uncompleted building could become a
vast and continually changing collage on the theme of
urban life in which a disembarking traveller might
participate. The grandeur and crudity of popular
broadsheets around 1830, and the way in which they
were pasted on to walls and hoardings of empty sites
and on top and on all sides of each other, probably
helped to prepare the ground for imagining and
accepting the graphic techniques of superimposition,
collage and montage which were to be used within the
particular poster itself at a later stage in its own
evolution. When the proliferation of posters occurred in
towns and cities, in the streets, there were some curious
developments; one was the use of dozens of the same
poster pasted in rows, notably in some of the
presidential elections in Latin America. In this case the
poster was called upon to mime a gesture of mass
support for the name and face of a candidate. An
unusually long and narrow format has sometimes also
been used for pasting on to drainpipes, when all the

walls were occupied, in the nightclub regions of Paris. In an urban jungle posters are sometimes torn down or have their message subverted by the addition of anonymous graffiti or those fly-by-night printed stickers which announce protest meetings; in such circumstances the poster supplies a background in which the intrusive message may be noticed. The inscription *Defense d'Afficher* (Billposting forbidden) and the invocation of the law of 1881 on public buildings and monuments in Paris meant that they are part of the urban sign language of history, just as the traffic signs are part of the operative sign language for traffic control. The monument and the traffic sign, both belonging to different types of discourse, have to be separated from the dynamic and unpredictable character of the poster. Public buildings and monuments signify a historic continuity; traffic signs signify the technical control of movement in the streets. Posters signify the day-to-day intrusion of popular needs, enthusiasms and events. The idiom of the poster changes, like slang, from time to time given new forms by idiosyncratic artistic invention, using technical processes. Sometimes the essence of the message lies in the witty juxtaposition of word and picture or in a well-conceived informational structure; perhaps most effectively by a simple memorable emblem. The poster lives on the streets and for this reason it also becomes a valuable historical document in a museum. Near Piccadilly at the corner of Hyde Park there is a large house, recently occupied by squatters, and it still carries a slogan which nobody has bothered to erase: 'We are the writing on your wall'.

After the October Revolution of 1917 in Russia, an immense quantity of posters appeared, and they varied also in their visual idiom (more than 3,000 are listed in *Sovetskii Plakat*, for the period 1918–1921). It is not surprising that we can recognise the flavour of expressionism, *art nouveau* or the rhetorical emphasis of the journalistic cartoon in many of them. The theme is revolutionary although in some cases the surviving conventions of calligraphic signatures, ornamental details and illusionistic representation remind us that here the visual language of a period is being used, not unlike that which was being used elsewhere for boosting commerce, recruitment and so forth. In September 1919, however, there appeared a new kind of poster, whose use is said to have been invented by Mikhail Cheremnykh, and known in the beginning as the 'Satire window of the Russian Telegraph Agency'. At this time the Russian Telegraph Agency had its name abbreviated to ROSTA (the equivalent of TASS today). Slogans, instructions, poetry were all in turn, boldly combined with graphic emblems and figuration, usually in sequence. The new idiom of the revolutionary poster is apparent.

Mikhail Cheremnykh
Rosta No. 497 1920

Many of the ROSTA windows were by the artist and poet Mayakovsky, who provided pictures and text for at least nine of the very first series, at a time when the format was designed for each shop window individually with no duplication, numbers 1–21 (September 1919 till February 1920), consisted of 2, 3, 4 or more poster units of different content; the windows in which they were placed were the windows of empty shops and vacant business premises. A typical ROSTA structure would consist of 4, 6, 8, 12 or 14 narrative pictures and captions or verses applied by stencil. It might be worth noting that with serigraphy or silk-screen printing, a more sophisticated stencilling technique is used on the colour screens. It is possible that the popular response to the narrative strip element of the ROSTA window may have grown from a familiarity with the *lubok*, a Russian picture-and-text, street literature, which survived until the beginning of this century. The ROSTA format for presenting information and instruction in political, military and economic matters appears as the revolutionary and environmental development of a typical folk tradition. Camilla Gray,

in *The Great Experiment: Russian Art 1863–1922*,
mentions the influence of both the sacred ikon and the
lubok in the paintings of Goncharova and Larionov
between 1908 and 1913. The author also states that: 'It
was during this summer and the following year (1909)
that the Burliuk brothers, following Larionov's
example, began working in a style less identified with
the French school, and with a growing interest in
incorporating national folk-art traditions'. And later:
'David Burliuk made friends with Mayakovsky and
together they began to devote themselves to poetry,
both of them trying to incorporate the previous years'
experience as painters . . .'. With the Revolution the
contours of 'poetry' or 'painting' became fused and
integrated to give a new meaning to the environment
(the street) or the transportation system (the railway).
After February 1920, simultaneously in different
localities several copies of the more successful ROSTA
posters were exhibited and identified by number
(ROSTA No XX). According to Cheremnych: 'The
reproductions were carried out with lightning speed';
upon receipt of an original, there existed fifty copies by
the following day, a few days later a whole edition (of
300 copies) would be completed. The stencil cutter
usually worked with his family or a small 'collective'
and the first copies to be made were immediately
forwarded to the most distant ROSTA branches; those
in the Moscow region being the last to receive their
quota. Later on duplicate sets of cardboard stencils were
forwarded on to the various localities to multiply the
edition in that region once again. It was discovered that
the emphatic numbering also maintained the
expectation and interest of viewers who would
inevitably look forward to the next poster to appear in
that particular window, when its theme would be
carried on and 'opened out like a window' as Wiktor
Duwakin states in *ROSTAFENSTER – Majakowski als
Dichter und bildender Künstler* (Dresden 1967). In
connection with the 'window' concept of projecting
information into the street, two designs for newspaper
buildings (the *PRAVDA* project by A. Vesnin and the
RADJENKO SELO project for Kiev) both have glass
screens, two floors in height, for a blown-up projection
of the front page news, to be changed each day.
During the twenty-nine months from September 1919
until February of 1922 more than 1,600 different

Project for *RADJENKO SELO*
newspaper building in Kiev
with glass screen for projecting
front-page news

ROSTA posters appeared in their windows and in railway stations and other premises. The simple stencil-cut adaptability and team-work used to produce these narrative posters corresponded to the collective creative work on the 'Agit-prop' or Agitation-Instruction trains; in both cases projection or diffusion of revolutionary propaganda by every available technique was at the same time used to give a new semantic interpretation to an existing element of transition or transportation (window or railway train). That those who were making the Revolution should give a revolutionary baptism to environment and means of transportation was logical, insofar as a particular place or piece of rolling stock would be a reminder of the society which had produced it. In England social evolution occurs through metamorphosis; when something disappears suddenly, like the last tramway, tears are shed (an Italian Futurist would find more poetry in the first tram's swaying movements). J. V. Stalin, in *Concerning Marxism in Linguistics* (Moscow 1950), has something to say about the semantics of the railway: 'At one time there were "Marxists" in our country who asserted that the railways left to us after the October Revolution were bourgeois railways, that it would be unseemly for us Marxists to utilise them, that they should be torn up and new "proletarian" railways built. For this they were nicknamed "troglodytes" . . . It goes without saying that such a primitive-anarchist view of society, of classes, of language has nothing in common with Marxism'.

Springtime poster by
Stenberg brothers

Evgeni Zamyatin, in *On Literature, Revolution and Entropy* (Moscow 1924), emphasises the nature of creative renewal when he states: 'The broad highway of Russian literature, worn shiny by the giant wheels of Tolstoy, Gorky, Chekhov, is realism, real life; consequently we must turn away from real life. The rails, sanctified and canonised by Blok, Sologub, Bely, are the rails of symbolism – symbolism which turned away from real life; consequently we must turn toward real life.

'Absurd, isn't it? The intersection of parallel lines is also absurd. But it is absurd only in the canonical, plane geometry of Euclid; in non-Euclidian geometry it's an axiom.'

An idiom changes within a historical context, accumulating its new words and images, frequently rediscovering others in its popular linguistic tradition, to correspond to the new situation; in this process it discards those which are obsolete. J. L. Borges, in *The Speech of Buenos Aires*, comments on this and says: 'The English language has not been pushed into a corner by slang', and elsewhere: 'the "wealth" of a language can be a euphemistic term for its death'. The first phase of the revolutionary poster idiom in Russia was typified by the ROSTA pattern, corresponding in execution and distribution to the immense creative effort of propaganda and education carried out during the civil war.

The phase which followed was typified by montage, technical experiment and the work of Lissitzky, Rodchenko, Klutsis and others. In the *New Left Review*, No 41, an essay on 'The Future of the Book' by El Lissitzky conveys some idea of the creative climate of these first two phases of the Revolution: 'The new movement which began in Russia in 1908 bound painter and poet together from the very first day . . . they did not produce select, numbered, de luxe editions, but cheap unlimited volumes, which today we must treat as popular art despite their sophistication.

In the Revolutionary period a latent energy has concentrated in the younger generation of our artists, which can only find release in large-scale popular commissions. The audience has become the masses, the semi-literate masses. With our work the Revolution has achieved a colossal labour of propaganda and enlightenment. We ripped up the traditional book into single pages, magnified these a hundred times, printed them in colour and stuck them up as posters in the streets . . . ours were not designed for rapid perception from a passing motor-car, but to be read and to enlighten from a short distance.' Three paragraphs further on he writes that: 'With the advent of the period of reconstruction in 1922, the production of books also rose rapidly. Our best artists seized on the problem of book production. At the beginning of 1922, I and the writer Ilya Ehrenburg edited the periodical *Vesch-Gegenstand-Objet* which was printed in Berlin. Access to the most developed German printing

Spartakiada photomontage in a poster by Klutsis 1928

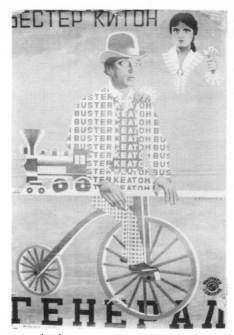

Two film posters by the
brothers Stenberg.
left: for Buster Keaton in
The General
right: for *Earth* by Dovchenko

techniques enabled us to realise some of our ideas about
the book. Thus we printed a picture-book *The Story of
Two Squares* . . . and the Mayakovsky-Book . . .'.

In the phase of reconstruction, the idiom of the poster
captured attention by its dynamism, but demanded a
more sophisticated awareness of the creative climate. It
showed its affinity with the new typographic design of
books and exhibitions, with architectural structure,
theatre design and with the techniques of the cinema.
Even before the unequalled creative genius of S. M.
Eisenstein became known, a group directed by Dziga
Vertov had published a manifesto in 1919 in support of
the documentary film, outlining the principles of what
is now called *'cinéma-vérité'*, and at that time known as
'cinéma-oeil' by those who received it favourably in
Paris. The athletic games poster 'Spartakiada' by G.
Klutsis (1928) synchronises by its montage of
documentary photography and text, recreating an
event, as would be done by the montage in the
diachronic structure of a film. Two posters by the
brothers Stenberg, for the Buster Keaton film *The
General* and *Earth* by Dovchenko, make use of
symbolic resonance rather than dynamic structure. In
these two posters figuration and sign are combined to
recall the tradition of the Russian ikon.

Peter and Mary Mayer have helped in the documentation of this text.

From the catalogue for *Art in Revolution*, Arts Council, 1971.

We may pick up a book, read it and then the book can lay hold of us. While it is being written its impetus and the form it takes can bend the author's will. Cervantes made his own helplessness quite plain with gentle irony when he wrote *Don Quixote*. He creates the characters and the situation, but they attain reality and get the upper hand. They make comments on his predicament and on his writing. Early in the first part the parish priest and the barber with some compassion allow one of his early works to survive their scrutiny. At the end of the second part Don Quixote freed from his madness as he dies, asks anyone present who may have the luck to meet the author, to ask him to excuse the many great absurdities which have caused the book to be written. Don Quixote is as vague about this author's name as Cervantes is vague about the name of that place in La Mancha where Quixote lived; to quote the opening lines '. . . the name of which I do not wish to remember.'

Cervantes is modern in his awareness of the book becoming that thing, that medium which it is. He confronts illusion with reality, grandiloquent romance with an absurd dusty picaresque experience. This was also Shakespeare's time and both writers died in the year 1616. Shakespeare examined and commented upon his medium through his characters; he also put a play inside a play as Cervantes put his book inside the book. In the shadowy library of the old hidalgo, Cervantes saw a collection of recipes for alienation. Hearing the sombre arrogant language of the epic dreams he added another volume to the shelves, but in it there is the sharp daylight of colloquial speech.

Three hundred years after Cervantes, Charles Péguy in the *Cahiers de la Quinzaine*, repeatedly questioned the reading habit, the way in which the print makes us lose our contact with life. In the past, according to Péguy: 'illiterates read the book of nature, or rather they themselves were that book, the book of creation.' In the *Note Conjointe sur M. Descartes*,[1] an unfinished text published after his heroic death in action in 1914, he compared modern literacy to a weary memory or a daily newspaper continuously overprinted with prefabricated slogans. Péguy was incapable of despair and he made continuous demands upon the honesty of his readers; he believed that to do the job properly 'each

1. Charles Péguy, *Note conjointe sur M. Descartes.* NRF Gallimard 1924.

Claude Oudeville who handset and printed each page of *Le Silence de la Mer*, during the German occupation of Paris.

photograph by Robert Doisneau

cahier should displease at least one-third of the subscribers.' For Péguy a book meant a total commitment to social and spiritual truth, it meant a refusal to be harnessed to an organised opinion-group. A book meant writing, editing, printing, proof correcting, publishing and even opening a bookshop in the Rue de la Sorbonne, which in turn became a forum for discussion and an outpost of Dreyfusism. By writing in defence of Dreyfus (*La Revue Blanche* 15th September 1899) Péguy made the little bookshop a target for the fanatical rage of the followers of the Anti-Semitic League and their street gangs.

Péguy, aware of the reader reading, wrote as he would speak with warmth and humanity, transcending material things and using simple language developing out of his inherited oral tradition, the vivid speech of his peasant grandmother who had never learnt to read. At the Ecole Normale Supérieure he attended the lectures of Bergson who later on admitted that Péguy understood his essential ideas as he would have wished to express them. For Péguy it was the living present which mattered; he did not look upon books as passports to a literary fame. In *Clio 11 (Dialogue de l'Histoire et de l'Ame Païenne)* there are some lines on the situation of the reader: 'We are so crammed with work, so stuffed with scruples, our conscience is so filled with guilt that we only read things related to our work. Because of this it is only when we are ill that we can, for a time, recover the capacity to be a reader, a true reader, who wants to read . . .' and further he continues: 'entering into a text means collaborating with its author, and this sort of reading is an act which is common to the reader and to the author. When it takes place, the text fulfils its destiny.'

The concept of a close relationship between author and reader ('. . . the text fulfils its destiny') in *Clio 11*, is in keeping with the concept of the book as a piece of team work. This is evident in an early work, *Jeanne d'Arc*, in which the names of all those involved in it, compositors, proof correctors and others, were recorded in the edition. In France many texts by Péguy fulfilled their destiny during the years, 1940–45, of the German occupation. His thought, his way of life and his works were an inspiration to the French Resistance Movement. The *Imprimeries Clandestines*, the clandestine presses in Paris, in Lyon, in Toulouse were the team work of writers, printers, bookbinders and their friends who then undertook the dangerous task of distribution, usually by bicycle.[2] In 1940 Jacques Decour and Politzer had founded the *Pensées Libre* which was to include contributions that were not purely propaganda; the copy for the second issue was in preparation for the press when they were raided by the Gestapo. One text survived because it had been delayed. This was *le Silence de la Mer* by 'Vercors', an engraver by profession who had some experience in book design. With Mme Desvignes they began the publication of the *Editions de Minuit*, with *le Silence de la Mer* as the first volume; 25 volumes were published during two and a half years. The printer Claude Oudeville hand set, printed and redistributed the type for each page during the two-hour lunch break in his workshop; the sheets were folded and stitched in the kitchen of the Desvignes apartment and the covers were pasted on by Vercors. In February 1942 the 350 copies of this first volume of the *Editions de Minuit* began to circulate. Jacques Decour was arrested on the eve of the day when printing of *le*

2. Vercors, Desvignes, Jean Cassou & others, *Imprimeries Clandestines. La Pointe* 1945.

Silence de la Mer was completed. He was shot three months later, in May 1942.

The *Editions de Minuit* represents the limited edition with an unlimited circulation; these books were continuously read and passed from one reader to the next. A number of copies of each edition were sold to cover production costs and the rest were then distributed free. The first four volumes, produced by hand were in editions of a few hundred copies, but in 1943 a large stop-cylinder machine was made available by E. Aulard who worked on it with his foreman Doré, on Saturdays and Sundays, after receiving the linotype composition of the texts; with the aid of Vasseur a bookbinder, the quantity of each edition was increased to more than a thousand copies. The editors were never short of texts which sometimes were brought from Toulouse or Lyon, or from abroad or even overseas; the bicycle continued to be the most reliable means of transporting paper and metal and also in distributing the books afterwards.

When Dr Samuel Johnson defined a book as a volume in which we read or write, he was probably including in his definition both the notebook with blank pages and also the printed volume with, as was the custom, margins ample enough for annotation. In the definition there is the implied point of view of the critic and the scholar for whom the book is an instrument of learning capable of absorbing additional ideas and observations in the form of notes. Even if we have no intention of using a book in this way, our attitude is influenced by the great familiarity and pervasiveness of paper in our day-to-day experience. Part of our freedom and sense of intimacy with books derives from a continuous use of the substance from which they are made.

The cultural diffusion of books is the outcome of a purely Chinese invention. During the Later Han Dynasty (105 AD) paper was invented by Ts'ai Lun, and in the early centuries of our era a variety of papers were made from hemp, plant fibres, cellulose and rags; writing paper, wrapping paper, even paper napkins and toilet paper were used. In *The Invention of Printing in China and its Spread Westwards*, T. F. Carter gives an account of the earliest known paper, found by Sir Aurel

Stein in the watch tower of the Great Chinese Wall: 'Rag paper, supposed till 1885 to have been invented in Europe in the fifteenth century, supposed till 1911 to have been invented by the Arabs of Samarkand in the eighth century, was carried back to the Chinese of the second century, and the Chinese record, stating that rag paper was invented at the beginning of the second century, was confirmed.' Elsewhere in his own review of T. F. Carter's book, Joseph Needham confirms the crucial time of transmission towards the West, in the year 751 when Arabs captured Chinese paper makers in Central Asia; 'after that, paper was being made in Baghdad in 793, Spain in 1150, Italy in 1276, Germany in 1391 and England in 1494.' As early as the fourth century BC a proto-paper called *hsi-t'i,* had been made by beating out matted waste floss silk in water and Ts'ai Lun, who was an inspector of public works, proposed in his report that cheaper ingredients such as tree bark, hemp, rags and fish nets should be used instead. In the latter part of the Han time (206 BC–220 AD) much scientific work and invention in astronomy, chemistry, botany and zoology was being written and copies were in demand; the invention of paper was necessary to diffuse knowledge.[3]

The oldest Chinese books were handwritten on bamboo strips, perforated and tied with cords of silk or thongs of leather to form a lattice bundle. The system was in use for more than a thousand years (*c.* 1300 BC–300 AD), although the earliest existing examples are those written or edited by Confucius (551–479 BC) including the *Book of Odes* and the *I-Ching* or *Book of Changes.* Bamboo books were heavy and their thongs became worn and broken with use. A more portable type of book was the silk scroll which came into use in the fourth century BC. When silk was made exclusively for books, ruled lines were woven into the fabric. The manufacture of silk for writing and for books, introduced one of the fundamental requirements in book production, namely the use of a standard metrification. Pieces of silk of the first century have been found with the width marked in decimal units and it is known that bolts of silk were used for the payment of taxes. In *Chinese footmeasures of the Past Nineteen Centuries,* Wang Kuo-Wei states that 'the standard of value was the *p'i* (bolt) which was required to measure

3. See also Liu Kuo-Chun, *The story of the Chinese Book.* Peking 1958.
4. A. E. Berriman, *Historical Metrology.* Dent 1953.

شَـــرح نَوّی چرب جے فی سَائِك بِنْ شُو
بنی وَبیاں آنک دَذَ انَك جِنَك نس معمّاید که انّوی باند انجِ جَعَاتِ
وُسْلِی وَنَسَایَهٔ

Chinese pulse-lore diagram incorporated into an Arabic text

40 *ch'ih* in length and 2 *ch'ih* 2 *t'sun* in width.' (30 feet by 19.8 inches; the *ch'ih* in this instance measuring 9 inches).[4] In ancient China there was another *ch'ih* used for bronze knife money and to measure a man's height (mentioned by Confucius). During the transition from silk to paper via the waste floss silk substance, it appears that the *shih ch'ih* of 12.53 inches became the standard paper width for scroll books.

Block printed books were probably invented during the Tang dynasty in the province of Szechuan; the earliest known example is the *Diamond Sutra* (868 AD) in the British Museum, but printed Buddhist scriptures must have been in circulation before the year 845 when Buddhism was banned by the Emperor T'ang Wu Tsung. In the tenth century State printing was sponsored by Wu Chao-I and later under the prime minister Feng Tao the great work of editing and printing the classics was carried out over a period of twenty-one years until in 953 the collection of one hundred and thirty volumes was completed. The establishment of the Sung Dynasty in 960 marked the beginning of the most important period in printing. An edition of 5000 volumes of the Buddhist scriptures, the *Tripitaka*, was published. Later in 1019 this was followed by one of the Taoist scriptures in 4565 volumes. Li Fang a minister of the Sung Emperor T'ai-tsung published the first encyclopedia in 978 and this was followed by the publication of books by others who dealt with specialised subjects such as agriculture, engineering or architecture. A Neoconfucian spirit of investigation typified this period. After the seventh century when a number of dictionaries had been published, the scroll-type book became obsolete; the rolling and unrolling of the paper length was inconvenient for works of reference and a pleating system was invented so that the format was folded rather like a computer print-out. Afterwards the 'Whirlwind binding' was introduced with a folded cover sheet pasted onto the first and last leaf. The typical Chinese book, light and flexible in its slip case has evolved from the 'butterfly' and 'wrapped back' forms used from the tenth to the fifteenth centuries. In the West the lack of an invented substance like paper and the continued use of animal skins for parchment and vellum meant that until paper mills were set up the

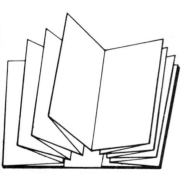

Chinese whirlwind binding

book remained a luxury article only within the reach of a privileged social class; there are incidents in the life of St Francis of Assisi showing his awareness that poverty and books could not co-exist at that time. The attitude of St Francis towards books can be seen to express his rejection of their costly material nature when he taught '. . . as for books, to look for their inwardness, not to their price.'[5]

The invention of paper became known to the West through the Moorish conquests in Spain but the invention of printing made its westward way along another route, as the Moslem world refused to put its literature into printed form; block-printed playing cards were probably brought back by Marco Polo and examples of, or information about, moveable type, invented by Pi Sheng during the Sung dynasty, may have arrived in the same way.

Books according to Jérôme Peignot are in essence the 'meeting place' of an author and each and every one of the readers. This meeting sometimes becomes a struggle. If there is peace and understanding the book and the reader can become an island, in the middle of a crowd. The book expands out of a closed structure into a sequence of leaves which refer to each other as we read; and we read at our own pace. Young children, learning to read, often embrace their books and handle them with signs of affection and some grown-up readers have admitted to an equivalent response.

The kinetic nature of reading is not merely due to the scanning movement of the eyes travelling over the text and the hands turning the pages upon which the text is distributed; there are also the normal shifting movements of the reader, sometimes modified by a response to what is being read. Anyone who has studied the design of a chair knows that there is no such thing as a single comfortable sitting posture for any particular chair. Comfort is found in a variety of continuously modified positions within the typical postural pattern schematised by the design of a given chair. A study in the applied ergonomics of reading has been carried out in the Typography Unit of the University of Reading. Under the direction of Michael Twyman, the research was made by Sister Sarah Clarke as a time and motion

5. St Francis of Assisi, *The Mirror of Perfection*. David Nutt 1900.

study of children reading.

Film sequences used to study reading behaviour are valuable because the book and the reader are to be found in duration rather than in time (as recorded by clocks) which is the reason why we lose ourselves in a good book.

Benjamin Lee Whorf in *Language Thought and Reality* made several comparisons between the Western concept of time and that of the Hopi Indian: 'To us, for whom time is a motion on a space, unvarying repetition seems to scatter its force along a row of units of that space, and to be wasted. To the Hopi, for whom time is not a motion but a 'getting later' of everything that has ever been done, unvarying repetition is not wasted but accumulated. It is storing up an invisible change that holds over into later events . . . Hopi may be called a timeless language. It recognises psychological time, which is much like Bergson's 'duration', but this 'time' is quite unlike the mathematical time, T, used by our physicists.' Time interpreted as a 'getting later' is also to be found in the second part of *Martin Fierro* (1879) by José Hernández. In that epic poem the gaucho making his reply in the verse contest, says 'time is but a delaying of what has got to be'.

Books are a repetition and an accumulation. *Biblion* for the Greeks of antiquity meant an accumulation of writing, a scroll or a book and the word derived from Byblos, a place north of Damascus which gave its name to that substance which it exported, the inner bark of the papyrus plant. Eventually *biblion*, the book, in the Christian world came to mean one single book, the Bible, the essential book.

Reading behaviour of two children. Line drawings of filmed sequences by Sister Sarah Clarke.

Icographic 1973
Dialogos 1979, translation by Jorge Perez-Román

Catalogue

Works are listed chronologically and are in the
collection of the artist unless otherwise stated.
Dimensions are given in centimetres, height before
width.

1 *Sleeper* 1943
oil on canvas, laid on board
25 × 29.5
Julio and Maureen Rotondi

2 *The Table* 1943
oil on canvas laid on board
60 × 39.7
Michael Stroud

3 *Woman and bath* 1947
oil on canvas 51 × 41
David and Anna Yandell

4 *Two More* 1947
aquatint 17.5 × 13.5

5 *Man with cigarette* 1947
oil on canvas 28 × 23

6 *Pilgrims* 1947
oil on board 20.5 × 20.5
Walter and Sue Turton

7 Fourteen monotypes illustrating
Max Jacob's
Le Cornet à dés 1947–8
each sheet 32.5 × 23.5

8 *Bunsen burners c* 1947–8
ink and gouache 37.2 × 24

9 *Hooks and discs c* 1947–8
gouache 38 × 45.5
Christopher Leyne

10 *Gas Ring* 1948
reed pen and ink, three drawings,
each 18.7 × 24

11 *Praliné* 1949
pen and ink 17.5 × 20
Michael Stroud

12 *Dancers* 1949
brush and ink 31.5 × 24
Michael Stroud

13 *Company Director's Wife* 1949
reed pen and ink 33 × 25.4
Michael Stroud

14 *The Cage* 1949
oil on canvas 51 × 40.5
David and Anna Yandell

15 *The Cage* 1950
oil on canvas 61 × 51
Mr and Mrs S. W. Dawson

16 *The Cage V* 1950
oil on canvas 122 × 96.5
Carol and Edwin Taylor

17 *The Keys* 1951
oil on canvas 41 × 35.5
Patricia Robertson

18 *Keys c* 1951
oil on canvas 60.5 × 45
Joseph Rykwert

19 *The Beach* 1952
oil on canvas 51.3 × 41.5
David and Anna Yandell

20 *Whitstable* 1955
ink and crayon 32.7 × 33
Private Collection

21 *at a* 1955 cut down and repainted
1969
oil on board prepared with pumice
powder
112.3 × 112.3

22 *Spectators* 1956
oil and printing ink on board
68.5 × 45
Patricia Robertson

23   three photograms from ink
     frottages 1956
     each 50.7 × 38.4
     Joseph Rykwert

24   *Matches* 1956
     frottage 48.5 × 36.5
     Mr and Mrs Brian Housden

25   *Spectators: Crowd* 1957
     oil and printing ink on board
     86 × 53
     Mr and Mrs Brian Housden

26   *Spectators: Wedding Guests* 1957
     oil on board 140 × 86.5
     Mr and Mrs Brian Housden

27   *The Anonymous* 1957
     oil and printing ink on board
     86.5 × 53.5
     Patricia Robertson

28   *Nonsense Conversation* 1957
     collage 61 × 45.5
     Mr and Mrs Brian Housden

29   *Formalities* 1957
     collage 53 × 53
     Private Collection

30   *Dialogue* 1957
     polyester resin and glass fibre, oil
     43 × 43
     Mr and Mrs Brian Housden

31   *Dialogue* (negative version) 1957
     polyester resin and glass fibre
     43 × 43
     Joseph Rykwert

32   *Troya* 1957
     polyester resin and fibre glass
     86.5 × 68.5
     Christopher Leyne

33   *Touch* 1958
     embossed sugar aquatint
     59.3 × 42.2 (plate)

34   *Conversation pieces* 1958
     soft ground etching and collage
     60 × 42.2

35   *Four Elements* 1958–9
     oil on board prepared with pumice
     powder
     139.2 × 139.2
     Joseph Rykwert

36   *Stele* 1959
     polyester resin and fibre glass
     106.5 × 66
     Private Collection

37   *Site* 1959
     oil on canvas 91.3 × 71.3
     Mr and Mrs Brian Housden

38   *Structure* 1959
     oil on canvas 91.4 × 71.1
     Brian Glover

39   *Travelling* 1959
     collage 61 × 43
     David and Anna Yandell

40   *Composition I* 1961
     brush and ink 52 × 48 (image)
     Christopher Leyne

41   *Composition II* c 1961–2
     brush and ink 59 × 51 (image)

42   *La Perezosa* 1962
     brush and ink 44 × 43.5

43   *Watercolour I* 1962
     watercolour 40.5 × 39 (image)

44   *Watercolour II* 1963
     watercolour 39.5 × 39 (image)

45   *Watercolour III* 1963
     watercolour 40 × 38.5

46   *Kuriquinga* 1963
     woodcut 35.5 × 25.5 (block size)

75   *Swamp* 1981
     watercolour 63 × 51.5

76   *Bicycle* 1981
     watercolour 63 × 51.5

77   *Near Ickleton* 1981
     watercolour 33 × 33 (image)

78   *El Murciélago* 1981
     collage 49.5 × 35.5

79   *Cambridge Gardens* 1982
     watercolour 63 × 51.5

80   *Rudiments* 1982
     stencilled oil on tea chest plywood
     40.5 × 33

81   *Catalpa Tree* 1983
     watercolour 61 × 47.5

82   *Figures* 1984
     stencilled oil on plywood
     25.2 × 35

83   *Codex atorrantis* 1984
     twenty four pages handprinted on
     brown ribbed
     kraft paper 25.5 × 25.5

The exhibition also includes material relating to the following design work:

architectural lettering

Standard Catalogue Company stand at the Building Exhibition, Olympia, 1955; display lettering and ceiling. Architect: Theo Crosby.

'House of the future' at the Ideal Home Exhibition, 1956; lettering. Architects: A. and P. Smithson.

Architectural Association Journal; lettering for a special issue, 1960.

International Union of Architects Congress and Exhibition buildings, South Bank, London, 1961; large multilingual coloured mural, and relief lettering. Architect: Theo Crosby.

Churchill College, Cambridge; foundation stone, 1961. Architect: Richard Sheppard.

Imperial College, University of London; heraldic plaques, 1963. Architect: Richard Sheppard.

Hinsley House (now Africa House), Covent Garden; lettering in relief, 1964. Architects: Lance Wright and Jaime Bellalta.

Ulster Museum, Belfast; lettering, 1965.

New Scotland Yard, London; environmental mobile sign, lettering and numbering system. Architects: John Taylor and Partners.

teaching

Typographic experiments by Ken
Garland, Germano Facetti and Edward
Wright made at the Central School of
Arts and Crafts, 1952–5.

'The interlocking kit', teaching project
at Cambridge University School of
Architecture, 1962–3.

'From a to z', foundation course project
at Chelsea School of Art, 1967.

posters and art exhibition work

'This is tomorrow', Whitechapel Art
Gallery, 1956.

'54/64 a decade of painting', Tate
Gallery, 1964 (in association with
Robin Fior).

'Art in Revolution', Hayward Gallery,
1971.

'Artists for Democracy: Cultural
Repression in Chile', symposium on
Latin American culture, Royal College
of Art, 1974.

'Dada and Surrealism Reviewed',
Hayward Gallery, 1978.

'New Painting – New York',
Hayward Gallery, 1979.

'Outsiders', Hayward Gallery, 1979.

'Film as Film', Hayward Gallery, 1979.

Lenders

Martin Colyer 60
Mr and Mrs S. W. Dawson 15
Brian Glover 38
Mr and Mrs Brian Housden 24, 25, 26, 28, 30, 37
Christopher Leyne 9, 32, 40
Teresa Matthews 58
Margaret and Trilokesh Mukherjee 54
Jorge Perez-Román 56
Patricia Robertson 17, 22, 27
Julio and Maureen Rotondi 1
Joseph Rykwert 18, 23, 31, 35, 59
Michael Stroud 2, 11, 12, 13
Carol and Edwin Taylor 16
Walter and Sue Turton 6
David and Anna Yandell 3, 14, 19, 39, 72
Private Collections 20, 29, 36, 73
*Department of Typography and Graphic
Communication, University of Reading
and the artist*

Tour

Carmarthen, Henry Thomas Gallery
7 January to 25 January 1985

Leicester Polytechnic, Kimberlin Exhibition Hall
6 February to 2 March 1985

Cambridge, Kettle's Yard Gallery
17 March to 21 April 1985

Norwich School of Art Gallery
7 May to 1 June 1985

Oxford, Museum of Modern Art
16 June to 28 July 1985

Wrexham Library Arts Centre
3 August to 6 September 1985

ISBN 0 7287 0441 2
© Arts Council and authors 1985
catalogue designed by Edward Wright
exhibition organised by Michael Harrison
with Judith Kimmelman
photographs by Alan Bartram   Lance Browne
A. C. Cooper   Pat Crooke   Theo Crosby
Robert Doisneau   Euan Duff   Lynn Fishman
Lesley Hamilton   Tim Highmoor   Brian Housden
Stella Snead   Eileen Tweedy   John Webb

Printed in England by Staples Printers St Albans
Limited at The Priory Press